RECYCLED LOVE

MASTERING THE ART OF DOG RESCUE

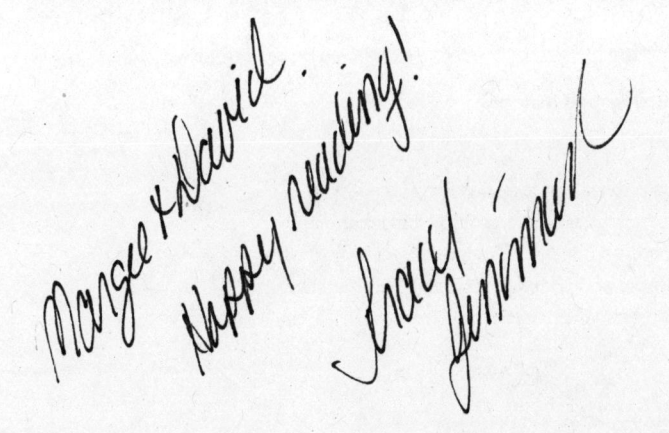

Margie & David,
Happy reading!
Tracy Jessiman

TRACY JESSIMAN

◆ FriesenPress

One Printers Way
Altona, MB R0G 0B0
Canada

www.friesenpress.com

Copyright © 2023 by Tracy Jessiman
First Edition — 2023

All rights reserved.

Photo credit to Elizabeth Andrews
Design by Frisesen Press

No part of this publication may be reproduced in any form, or by any means, electronic or mechanical, including photocopying, recording, or any information browsing, storage, or retrieval system, without permission in writing from FriesenPress.

ISBN
978-1-03-916218-1 (Hardcover)
978-1-03-916217-4 (Paperback)
978-1-03-916219-8 (eBook)

1. PETS, DOGS

Distributed to the trade by The Ingram Book Company

*This book is dedicated to
the organizations, volunteers, advocates, and veterinarians
who fiercely fight on behalf of rescue dogs.*

FOREWORD

I felt compelled to write this book to dispel the many misconceptions about rescue dogs. My goal is to prove that rescue dogs are not damaged; they have been let down by humans. Some dogs drift into rescue unharmed, as they may have come from loving, supportive homes. Others may have a difficult journey that leaves them needing more help, encouragement, and medical care. Every dog, no matter its past, is supported. And any dog that needs help, training, or extra love and attention will receive it from the rescue organization.

The book explains and illustrates how a rescue dog's journey to a rescue organization is not a simple straight line; it can be pretty complicated. Some dogs may have been dearly loved and given up voluntarily, but many come from sad or difficult situations. Yet, no matter the dog's background, the stories about redemption and devotion from the families who ensure their cherished rescue dog thrives will inspire you.

The book details the causes of homelessness for dogs and offers solutions. The book also explains why people get involved in animal advocacy and what to look for in a responsible rescue organization.

This book took two years to write, including conducting research and interviews, and the result is a one-of-a-kind book that gives the reader a behind-the-scenes view into the world of dog rescue.

The heartwarming rescue story about Max is an example of the wonderful rescue dogs highlighted throughout this book. His story shows the love, devotion, and lifetime commitment adopters make to their rescue dogs. Here is Max's story.

MAX

"Nobody has ever measured, not even poets, how much the heart can hold."
~Zelda Fitzgerald~

Max is a heart dog, a one-of-a-kind, soul-touching, unconditionally loved rescue dog. He's the dog his mom will spend the rest of her life comparing every other dog to, because Max has set the bar very high.

Max, a white Shepherd-mix boy, was adopted at nine months old by a kind, hyper-positive young veterinary technician. She was told Max had been surrendered to the rescue organization by an older couple, who said he was too much for them to handle. Max's new mom made a lifetime commitment to Max to deal with anything he would throw her way. She quickly discovered he had the worst case of separation anxiety she had ever encountered. But she made it her mission to ensure Max lived a long, well-balanced, fulfilled life, and she proudly accomplished her goal.

Max's mom said she knew he was a very gentle dog from the beginning. The first day she took him to an off-leash dog park, Max saw a little girl and bolted toward the child. He stopped short, gave the little girl a gentle lick on her cheek, and ran back to his mom, leaving the giggling girl behind. His mom said he was a fantastic dog from the beginning of their life together, and he had a naturally sweet and loving disposition.

When she adopted Max, she was in a long-term relationship, and when the union ended, Max left with his mom. When she moved across the country, Max was with her. When she met and fell in love with her soulmate, Max was with her. When she married her soulmate, Max was her bridesmaid. Years later, Max was with her when she found out she was expecting her first child.

She said Max was her lifeline during every transition in her life. Even with his severe separation anxiety, his devotion to her was undeniable. Because of his separation anxiety, she exercised Max as much as possible, took him for training and enrolled him in agility. Every Sunday, she prepared seven large red Kongs with wet dog food and cottage cheese and put them in the freezer. Max got one each day when she left the house for work.

Max's separation anxiety was so bad he chewed door frames, shoes, and even carpets. But she always said Max gave back more—that was the trade-off.

Sometimes Max went to doggy daycare during the day. If his mom had to work longer at the veterinary clinic, she'd pick up Max from daycare and bring him back to work with her. She did everything humanly possible to help Max with his separation anxiety, but little did she know that she would innocently stumble across his remedy, something that made his fear vanish.

Before they married, her partner said he wanted to get another dog. They adopted a sweet female chocolate Labrador retriever named Higbee. From the day Higbee moved in, Max's separation anxiety moved out. The dogs became inseparable. At the young couple's wedding, Max was the bridesmaid and Higbee the groomsman.

MAX

Max lived a long, fulfilling life, and this might not have happened if the sweetest veterinary technician hadn't adopted him. Dogs with separation anxiety struggle daily, and it's a horrible and brutal way for them to live. Luckily, Higbee sent all of Max's anxiety away, forever.

As the young couple embraced the pending birth of their first child with great excitement, Max became ill. They sadly lost Max one month before their son was born. The new mom wanted to honour her irreplaceable best friend; she gave their son the middle name of Maxwell. That is what a heart dog does to its family. Even though the couple now has two young children and two wonderful dogs, Max still takes up most of the space in his mom's heart. That is a heart dog.

TABLE OF CONTENTS

Foreword	v
Max	vii
Making a Rescuer	1
Creating a Rescue Dog	23
The Ugly Side of Dog Breeding	49
A Loving Forever Home	83
Finding a Responsible Rescue	107
Adopting a Special Needs Dog	131
Canine Covid Crisis	145
Talk Doggy to Me	153
Acknowledgments	171
Rescue Families	173
Tips for Finding a Responsible Rescue	175
Tips for Finding a Responsible Breeder	176
Acronyms & Definitions	177
Sources	179
About the Author	195

MAKING A RESCUER

"Remember that the happiest people are not those getting more, but those giving more."
~H. Jackson Brown, Jr.~

People often say, "It must be fun rescuing dogs." I can guarantee that dog rescue is not fun. Advocating on behalf of man's best friend is not for the weak. It takes a strong backbone, bravery, thick skin, and plenty of red wine. Dog rescue can be harsh, brutal, and downright savage. At the same time, it can be soul-finding and sometimes soul-breaking. Transporting a surrendered dog with a shattered spirit can leave you looking at the world with outrage. Witnessing a dog who has psychologically shut down because of abuse or negligence alters your perspective about humanity. Watching a homeless dog that finds your outstretched hand petrifying will scar you like nothing else.

The reality is that dogs become homeless because of human actions, inactions, or negligence. As humans have caused dogs to become homeless, we need to help them find permanent homes. We desperately need to help these dogs heal and move forward.

I have advocated for dogs in need for most of my adult life. I find dogs inspiring, entertaining, and downright fascinating. I hope to continue advocating on their behalf until my last breath, and I am not alone. Many extraordinary people have dedicated their lives to helping homeless dogs.

These advocates come from every walk of life, and their reasons for participating are just as varied. While researching my weekly column, I have interviewed politicians, city councillors, lawyers, individuals who operate rescue organizations, CEOs, children, and many volunteers. When I ask them why they feel the need to help homeless dogs, their reasons are diverse, unique, and personal.

Let's start with my story. My first experience with animal welfare began in my childhood when I heard about a dreadful dog abuse case. A man had put his family dog in a bag, tied it to the bumper of his car, and driven away, dragging the dog behind. When he was arrested, he told the officers he was trying to teach his dog to stop chasing cars. Unbelievably, the dog survived, and authorities found it a new home.

This abuse case was the first time I heard about a human harming a family pet, and it deeply affected the rest of my life. I was too young to comprehend why someone would hurt a defenseless animal. My siblings and I grew up with animals all around us, and we treasured our pets. We always had a dog in our home and every one of our dearly loved dogs came from the local dog pound.

Fast forward, I grew up and met my animal-loving husband while working at Merrill Lynch. About a year into our relationship, we heard about a horrific animal abuse case. I will not go into the graphic details, but it was a dogfighting bust by the police. Astonishingly, the dog survived. I called the rescue organization and offered our credit card to cover the dog's medical care, but funds had begun flowing in, so we donated.

During our marriage we have happily and generously donated much-needed funding to many rescue organizations, but the parade of homeless dogs never ended. We fostered, fundraised (in our home or at the yacht club), and volunteered our time to transport dogs, but it never seemed enough. I even donated 100% of the proceeds from my one-of-a-kind pet portrait paintings to rescues.

I started writing in a weekly newspaper and multimedia column about rescue and pet-related topics, and was offered airtime on two local radio stations. I highlighted homeless pets on their airwaves and had on-air discussions about animal advocacy or local abuse situations. Rescue organizations desperately need media support in every form (print, television, radio, and social media) to help bring awareness to animal rescue and advocacy efforts. Although these opportunities highlighted animal rescue endeavors, I still had a nagging feeling I wasn't doing enough to get the message out. What complicated my frustration was there seemed to be misinformation regarding animal rescue organizations and animal advocacy, so my husband strongly urged me to write a book.

I thought about the book for a long time and decided I would commit to writing it only if it proved to be unique. I wanted it to be an informative guide on how rescue organizations operate, where the dogs come from, and why people get involved. I wanted the book to be bursting with real-life rescue dogs thriving in their homes. Some of the dogs may have come from terrible situations, but they all flourished with the right balance of love and devotion. This devotion comes from the people who promised never to let them down, and they kept that promise at any cost.

As I moved through the utter bliss of the writing process, another feeling took over. I hoped the book would finally dispel many myths surrounding rescue dogs, rescue organizations, and animal advocacy. What also became apparent was the thought that someone may read the book and understand why so many people, such as myself, commit to rescuing, and that maybe the reader would want to become involved in the crusade. Perhaps, after reading the book, they would also understand why this mission is vitally important in our society and understand the determination and commitment of volunteers.

Dogs are the most forgiving animals on the planet, and they have always been vital to me, which is why I constantly worry about their welfare. They brought me great comfort as a child, the least I can do as an adult is advocate on their behalf. That's my story, but there are thousands of other tales about why people enter dog rescue. Everyone has a unique talent or special purpose—mine is advocating on behalf of rescue dogs.

THE HUMANITARIAN VETERINARIAN

If you were to ask a veterinarian if they considered themselves a rescuer, most would answer no. But in my personal experience, they are rescuers and they deserve to be recognized.

Most rescue organizations have an intimate relationship with a clinic, and that relationship is beneficial to both parties. If the clinic has a dog that a family can no longer care for, the clinic will reach out to the rescue after they have explained the options to the dog owner. Some people can no longer care for their dog for economic reasons, divorce, the birth of a child, or for other reasons. Clinics with a rescue relationship can offer help to the family.

On the other hand, if the same rescue organization has taken in a dog that needs veterinary care, the clinic will make room for that new dog. The clinic and the rescue organization support and aid each other.

The win-win for both parties is that the clinic is able to save the lives of dogs that may have otherwise been euthanized, and rescue groups have a place to take new or unknown dogs to find out whether the dog has any underlying health issues.

The last level of the relationship is also a success for both parties. Clinics will often offer a slight discount to rescue groups for veterinary care such as spaying, neutering, vaccinating, dental care, and other services. The discounts help the rescue organizations, as most work on a shoestring budget. Moreover, veterinarians understand that once the rescue dog is adopted, the dog may become a lifelong client at the clinic as a result of the veterinary care the dog received.

WHY PEOPLE BECOME INVOLVED IN DOG RESCUE

Some people become involved when they hear or read about an animal abuse situation that tugs at their heartstrings. They may become a dedicated foster home or volunteer at a shelter. They will do anything to help support animal rescue organizations that save dogs.

Single-parent families may want their children to have the experience of helping a dog that has been neglected. They may want their children to experience assisting an animal in need and learn about compassion for animals and humans, so they offer up their homes and become dedicated foster households. Rescues and shelters depend on these homes; they are the backbone of every organization's success.

Couples may become involved with rescues even though they do not have pets. Their careers or lifestyle may not allow time for owning a pet, so they volunteer at a shelter to help walk dogs or drive dogs to veterinary appointments. They may fundraise at their respective offices or volunteer to run an online auction. Many single individuals become involved for the same reasons.

Young children will often forgo gifts for birthdays and ask for donations to local animal rescue organizations instead. They may even have a weekend garage sale or lemonade and baked goods stand, with proceeds donated to an animal shelter.

PROFESSIONAL SPORTS TO THE RESCUE

Many professional sports teams try to help volunteer organizations raise much-needed funding. My husband has a lengthy hockey background, and he obtained an authentic Auston Matthews signed jersey from Toronto Maple Leaf's head coach Mike Babcock. We happily auctioned off the jersey with help from a local radio station. The funds were donated to an animal rescue organization, and the funds helped find many dogs loving homes.

NO REST FOR A DOG RESCUER

There is no magical formula to becoming an animal advocate; you only have to care. And that caring doesn't end solely with a rescue organization. Many people involved in dog rescue keep spare leashes and collars of different sizes in their vehicles. Rescuers often come across lost or wandering dogs. It's happened to my friends and to me multiple times over the years, and we either return the dog to its home, or place it with animal control if it doesn't have a dog license tag or microchip.

On one memorable occasion, I was driving to work early in the morning when I came across a dog running all over the road. Cars were slowing down to get around the dog, but no one stopped to help. I could also see an older man walking in the distance with a cane in one hand and a leash in the other. His young, exuberant German shepherd was playing a good game of keep-away and was in full play mode, with no intention of being caught.

I pulled my car off the road, grabbed a spare leash from the backseat, and jumped out to see if I could help. Younger dogs can be pretty nosey, so I took advantage of that instinct. I got the dog's full attention, and then I ran away from him, knowing he'd chase me. As the dog came up along my side, I grabbed his collar and clipped on my leash. He didn't struggle—he knew he was busted. The man who owned this majestic beast pointed out his laneway with his cane. I waited for him so I could help get the dog back into the house. The man and his wife were in tears and thankful that someone had safely captured their beloved dog.

They wanted me to stay for breakfast, but I was already late for work. I politely thanked them and started walking back down their long country driveway. I was surprised when I turned around and saw four tall, handsome men walking slowly and cautiously towards me. One of them gently asked if I was okay and said he would escort me back to my vehicle. I excitedly told him about my adventure, but the look of worry and concern on his face confused me until I saw my car.

I had jumped out of my car so quickly, I left the door wide open, the car's four-way lights were blinking, my purse had spilled out its contents, and my black patent high-heeled shoes were in the middle of the road. There were numerous cars and trucks pulled over, and some people were walking in the nearby field. These people thought I had been forcefully abducted from my car and were urgently looking for me. The man who walked me to my vehicle called 911 to tell them I was safe. I humbly thanked as many people as possible and drove off to work in my shredded nylons.

LOVE IS A FOUR-LEGGED WORD

Dog rescue never leaves you when you are an animal advocate. It's always with you, just like your heart. I have heard endless tales from people with feet on the ground, involved with rescue. These are people who stop traffic on highways because a dog is running on the road. People who search night and day to help find lost dogs. People who set large cage traps and wait through the night hoping to trap a dog that has not only been lost, but who is now in the "fight or flight stage" and is tough to catch. I've heard stories of individuals who drive to pick up a surrendered dog only to discover puppies or other dogs are also in the house. They will dedicate time to help the family or offer emotional assistance to surrender the other dogs. Advocates will often pay, out of their own pockets, for veterinary services or food for a family's dog when the owner is suffering financially.

MAKING A RESCUER

When you become an animal lover, it's with you for life. At any given time, that pure unadulterated love for animals comes screaming out, and this is what happened in the story about Crystal. Many people who didn't know each other came together to save this beautiful girl on the very last leg of her journey to her forever home.

CRYSTAL

"Live like someone left the gate open."
~unknown~

Crystal took the above quote to heart one day, and her story went viral worldwide. She is a rescued Podenco (Spanish hound) who took a British Airways flight from Spain to Canada. The flight arrived safely at Canada's Toronto Pearson International Airport, but when the crew opened the cargo hold, Crystal managed to escape. Her crate had not been correctly fastened, and at some point during the flight she got loose in the plane's storage area.

Traffic on the airport runway had to be halted for both arrivals and departures after two planes attempted to land but had to be diverted. It took thirteen hours, night vision goggles, CCTV (Closed Circuit Television), the control tower, a falconer (keeps birds off the runway), and extra staff brought in to finally locate Crystal. She ran nonstop around the runway until she eventually tired herself out and allowed someone to get her to safety.

MAKING A RESCUER

Crystal on *Fox News:* "Every dog has its day." https://fxn.ws/36GRYWN

This beautiful girl's life started when she was found as a puppy in Spain, living in a cave with two other pups and a female dog. It was later discovered the female dog was not the mother of the puppies. The animals were gently gathered up and taken to a well-respected animal shelter in Spain. This shelter has been devoted to saving Podencos and Galgos (Spanish greyhounds) for many years.

You may not be aware, but Spain has a poor reputation for the way they mistreat this intelligent breed of hunting dogs. The Spanish rescue saves the dogs and finds permanent loving homes worldwide. It is a responsible and ethical organization with a well-regarded reputation internationally.

Crystal's forever home is in Canada, and she landed in a household with a woman who has 25 years of experience in animal rescue. She and her husband have two other dogs that Crystal dearly loves.

This spunky girl is entirely motivated by food. So much so that, when she is waiting for her food bowl, she shakes in anticipation. She's cuddly, and she will crawl up on her mother's lap and get in her face for kisses. But when you look like Crystal, who wouldn't want to kiss that sweet face? She loves to be touched, which makes bathing and trimming her nails very easy. Her mother also said that Crystal is an immaculate girl, and she cleans herself as if she's a cat.

But Crystal is a bull in a china shop. She's clumsy and goofy, but very athletic. She can do a 360-degree turn in mid-air when she jumps. Luckily, her parents have a six-foot fence; otherwise, Crystal would clear it and search for treats.

I was told Crystal lives in a cemetery of destroyed stuffed animals, all destroyed by her, accidentally on purpose. But she still plays tug of war with the empty bodies with her fur siblings. The only toy she has not destroyed to date is an enormous giant red Kong, but there's hope. She's a slender, fit dog with a body made from pure muscle, with a beautiful, caring heart. She's athletic and active, yet her favorite little person in the whole world is the new baby (two-legged) granddaughter, and Crystal can't get enough of her. She kisses her and watches over her whenever she's in the house.

One of Crystal's favorite pastimes is watching kids outside. She loves going for walks and meeting new dogs. She loves chasing her fur siblings in the backyard, and she does zoomies, running past them. They are never able to catch up to her. She's a funny girl who can be a bit shy meeting new people but perks up as soon as a treat appears.

At the end of every day, she sleeps peacefully between her parents, most likely dreaming about that inflight dinner service she never received.

JAXSON

*"Age is an issue of mind over matter.
If you don't mind, it doesn't matter."*
~Mark Twain~

A lovely couple adopted Jaxson, a mixed-breed boxer who was ten years old. He was not their first dog. During their marriage, they have adopted seven dogs into their family. The couple is deeply entrenched in animal advocacy, and the husband is a past president of one of the largest rescue-advocacy organizations in the world. During his term, he transformed that organization and established one of the first no-kill mandates in North America. This couple understands rescue and are passionate about their mission. They are dedicated to supporting animal advocacy.

As a result of their dedication, they were sent a picture of Jaxson from the rescue organization. The shelter said Jaxson was a wonderful dog, but he didn't tick all the boxes for adoption, mainly because of his age. The couple had recently lost a beloved dog, and they were not sure they were ready to add to their family. Long story short, they put in an application and made the six-hour drive to meet Jaxson. The shelter insisted they bring their dog along for the meeting, so the family of three set off for the meet-and-greet.

When they arrived at the shelter, they were sad to hear there was a woman that also put in an application. The woman met Jaxson and had left the shelter to discuss the adoption with her husband. Disappointed but not giving up, the couple drove another 2.5 hours to their in-laws to await word regarding their application.

This couple understands the adoption application process, so they were more than patient waiting for the final decision. Happily, the shelter called them to say Jaxson was theirs if they were still interested. They sped back to the shelter and picked up handsome Jaxson. Funny, when Jaxson saw them, he had the look of, "Where have you been? I've been waiting for you!" all over his face. He jumped in the backseat with his new fur-sister and went to his forever home. It was love at first sight for the new family of four.

Adopting an older dog comes with risks, and this couple was more than willing to take on that risk with Jaxson. His adoptive mom said, "Right out of the gate, it's an emotional risk. Will we have him to love for six months? A year, maybe? No matter how long he would be with us, we were dedicated to loving him. But more importantly, he taught us how to live in the moment."

The first day they arrived home with Jaxson, he walked into the house and jumped up on the couch. He acted as if he had lived there all his life. He cuddled with his doggy sibling and slept between his mom and dad on the first night, and every night going forward. He was housetrained, socialized, well-mannered, and a complete joy to be around. They thought Jaxson must have been a well-loved family dog in his previous life, and they were right. He had been raised in a wonderful home but ended up at the shelter after both of his owners sadly passed away.

Bringing any adult rescue dog into your home must be done delicately. The adoptive dad knows that baseball-cap-wearing men can sometimes be a trigger. Therefore, he never wore a baseball cap around Jaxson. But when Jaxson met a cap-wearing friend for the first time, it was the complete opposite reaction for this rescue dog. Jaxson went wild in a hilarious way. He fell in love with their friend, and it wasn't a spring fling. He obsessed over the friend every time they got together.

One of Jaxson's favorite things was to go for a ride in his dad's truck. He was so obsessed with the rides that they had to spell the word "truck" because Jaxson lost his mind every time he heard the word. And if he was lucky enough to go to work with his dad, that was the best day ever, getting two rides in one day. He also loved going for walks and was very judgmental if they walked too slow or lollygagged behind. His mom also said he didn't just walk; he pranced.

Jaxson met a little toddler, and again, with a new dog, you need to be especially careful in case they are not fond of children. Well, Jaxson debunked that immediately. He followed the child all over the house as if it was the only person in the world. He was gentle, attentive, and affectionate with the child.

Jaxson lived two great years with his wonderful adoptive family, and they fondly remember him as their one-of-a-kind boy. They miss him dearly and smile when they find themselves spelling out the word "truck."

MOJO

"It takes nothing away from a human to be kind to an animal."
~Joaquin Phoenix~

Mojo isn't supposed to be here, but luckily, the world is a better place because of him. At three months old, he was surrendered from a backyard breeder. Tiny Mojo was severely dehydrated, on the brink of starvation, and suffering from a terrible case of demodectic mange. He was utterly furless, had difficulty walking, and the mange had progressed to the point that he was bleeding through his skin.

The rescuers immediately took Mojo to their local veterinarian. The doctor told them the puppy might not survive, and the next twenty-four hours would be critical. Although the little guy was starting to shut down, he improved a little, and the veterinarian decided to send Mojo to the veterinary hospital four hours away. He spent seven days in the hospital's care, and everyone fell in love with the sweet, pink puppy. Surprisingly, people worldwide followed Mojo's story on social media, and donations for his care came rolling in.

The Dodo (a media brand focused on telling animal stories) made a heartwarming video about Mojo reuniting with his adoptive dad: "Pit Bull Puppy Clinging to Life Reunites with Dad Who Rescued Him" | *The Dodo*: https://www.youtube.com/watch?v=QBulAnnxXow

The couple who initially took possession of Mojo had discussed opening a private animal rescue organization at length. That idea accelerated with one look at the sick puppy. Therefore, Mojo was the catalyst—their rescue organization was created nine years ago and continues today.

When Mojo returned from his lengthy stay in the hospital, the couple decided they couldn't part with him, so they adopted Mojo. They took terrific care of him, as he needed to take daily baths in a medicated soap, and he was on serious medication.

Mojo is extremely friendly and gentle, and he loves everyone. He shares his home with his fur brothers, and helps his parents tend to the animals they save. Mojo is perfect, except his fur never thickened as he matured. His coat is about a half of what it should be, but he reminds his parents, "I'm perfect; I don't shed like your other dogs." His loving parents look after him in every way a dog should be taken care of. In the summer, he needs sunscreen, and in the winter, he wears a coat. Mojo doesn't care about his missing fur because he knows his parents love him unconditionally.

Mojo often visits local schools to educate students about responsible pet ownership. He loves going because the school always has excellent treats, and the kids love to smother him with affection. Between naps on the couch, Mojo raises funds for his parents' rescue. He has an annual Christmas calendar and Christmas card fundraiser. He also has a Facebook page called "Help for Mojo." He has raised thousands of dollars in the last nine years, and he feels so proud to have helped so many homeless pets.

Mojo starts the average day at precisely 6:00 am when he wakes his mom up for breakfast. Of course, he has slept under the covers, as quiet as a little mouse, all night between his parents. He loves his food, all food, especially potato chips.

After potato chips or any meal, he burrows back under the blankets. When his mom walks by him, his tail thumps under the layers. She calls

Mojo her emotional baby who won't leave the couch until she kisses him and gives him belly rubs. This boy loves his aunties, and he knows them by name. He's very smart-alecky and flirty with the ladies, with his look of, "I'm so sweet, give me a kiss!"

And everyone wants to kiss Mojo because his story has resonated with the world. He has friends in Australia, France, and even New Zealand. People on world tours have even asked his parents if they can meet Mojo.

This particular boy has become a teaching tool about animal negligence, and a petition concerning animal rights was started because of him. Mojo takes it all in stride, he's just happy as long as he has his devoted parents beside him and they continue to give him potato chip treats.

CHARLIE

*"If you want others to be happy, practice compassion.
If you want to be happy, practice compassion."*
~Dalai Lama~

Charlie is a distinguished and dapper eleven-year-old purebred Australian Shepherd. He landed in a loving home with a woman who already had a wonderful rescue dog. It would not be untrue to say that the rescue dog already living in the home, rescued Charlie.

The first rescue dog became ill about a month after he was adopted. His veterinarian discovered he had Addison's disease. This is what the American Kennel Club says about Addison's disease:

"Addison's disease occurs when the adrenal glands fail to produce the hormones that they are in charge of in the body. The most important hormones produced by the adrenal glands are steroids, particularly aldosterone and cortisol. These steroids play a large role in regulating your

dog's internal organs and body systems. Without them, your dog's body deteriorates, leading to serious complications and even death."

The dog was put on medication, which saved his young life. There was little information about the disease at the time, so his mother, a retired nurse, did a deep dive into the research. She then created a Facebook group: "Addison Dogs - Canine Addison Disease." She has over 15,000 followers and has assisted many Addison-diagnosed dogs. One afternoon a man reached out to her for help. He had heard about a dog diagnosed with the disease (Charlie), and he was told the owners were going to euthanize the dog. He begged her to reach out to the dog owners, which she did, and Charlie was flown across the country to live with her.

Arrangements were made to collect Charlie at 4:00 am from the airport, and she had a local veterinarian on standby. Over the next few weeks, and with the help of medication, Charlie became a happy and healthy dog. He's on monthly injections for the rest of his life, which he takes like a pro, with a bit of peanut butter, of course.

If her other rescue dog had not been diagnosed with the same disease, and if his mom had not created the social media site, little Charlie might not be with us today.

Charlie loves food, hiking, car rides, swimming, cats, and hanging with any dog he meets. Sometimes, he is also the "fun police." Whenever a foster dog arrives in his home, he plays with them, but his fur brothers are off-limits. He comically puts himself in the middle of the fun, pushing the foster dog away. Charlie could probably get a full-time job with the local police or as a bouncer at a nightclub.

Charlie has one weakness, trips to the veterinarian. Although he loves car rides, Charlie's anxiety kicks in as soon as the car stops at the clinic. His mom does everything possible to support him, but he can't shake it off. At one of his appointments, he fainted from the stress. Luckily, his appointments are far and few between because other than his Addison's disease, he's a healthy boy. His ten-kilometer hikes with his mom have kept him in shape.

He's happiest at home with his fur brothers, his mom, his toys, the kitchen fridge, and his front window—so that he can bark at the world. His mom often reminds him how lucky he was to have a stranger reach out to her, halfway across the country, to help a little dog he had never met. Charlie appreciates his excellent fortune and repays the kind deed by supporting the many foster dogs that have spent time in his home over the years. Of course, the foster dogs must obey the rules and only play with him.

He sleeps in his mom's bed at night, by her feet, and does his mattress-travelling during the night. He's an affectionate, social boy who warms up to visitors by firstly ignoring them, then going in for a big kiss. This guy is all heart and is the essence of a well-mannered gentleman. He's James Bond in a doggy suit, and no one can resist him.

LOLLIE & DYSON

"It's tough to stay married. My wife kisses the dog on the lips, yet she won't drink from my glass."
~Rodney Dangerfield~

Lollie and Dyson were part of a litter of eleven puppies. An individual threatened to drown all the puppies if someone did not pick them up. A woman involved in rescue heard about the puppies and raced to save them. She split the puppies between two rescue organizations, and happily, the puppies were all healthy, and all of them were eventually adopted.

A married couple looking to adopt one puppy put in a powerful adoption application. The wife is an executive with a different rescue organization. When puppy volunteers checked her references, everyone said to give her whatever she wanted, as it would be a wonderful home for any puppy or dog.

They met the puppy they dearly wanted to bring home when they were approved for adoption. But the little male puppy had other plans. He was curled up tightly with his sister, and the couple couldn't bear to separate the two, so they adopted both pups.

MAKING A RESCUER

When they arrived home with the pups home, they picked the perfect names. Dyson, the male, was named after the famous vacuum because nothing hits the floor without Dyson capturing it, especially food. They called the female pup Lollie because they thought she was a lab-collie mix. But as she grew, they could tell she was part husky.

Outside of naming two gorgeous pups, the couple was prepared for "littermate syndrome," which is an actual condition, if you haven't heard about it. It manifests itself when littermates or puppies from different litters are brought home simultaneously. It can result in high anxiety when the two are separated, fear of unfamiliar people and noises, and refusal to eat alone. The dogs may bond closely with each other, but not with their humans. Some professional trainers strongly recommend against bringing two puppies into the same home simultaneously.

This couple was well-versed in this potential problem, and well-prepared for two puppies. They knew the puppies had very different personalities, and they nurtured that independence. They took the puppies to training classes separately. They ensured that the dogs had individual, quiet-time pens. They walked and fed them separately. The pups grew, quickly, into wonderful well-adjusted dogs with entirely different personalities.

Lollie is very independent and will only snuggle with her parents on her terms. She's a drama queen who loves to stick her nose up in the air and howl as loudly as possible. She sticks her nose so far upright she can almost touch her curled tail. Her tail curves upward like a typical Siberian husky. She will jump up on the couch for a cuddle, but her brother will likely start to poke at her. This makes her vocalize her displeasure, and she leaves, but she doesn't forget to get back at him. Outside, Lollie will torment Dyson by chasing him and stealing any toy he wants to play with. She acts like the typical two-legged older sister.

Dyson is very laid back and easygoing. He loves to chase the ball but will drop it if his sister wants it. He also watches television and gets very animated if an animal should appear on the screen, even cartoon animals. He'll bark at the TV, then walk around the house, mumbling under his breath. He's a handsome dude, so he may be upset he isn't on the TV screen. Maybe his parents should get him an agent. He's more attractive than Lassie, or at least he thinks so.

RECYCLED LOVE

To think these two almost didn't make it is astonishing. Luckily, there is always a kind and compassionate rescuer looking out for dogs in need of saving, just like their mom. Lollie and Dyson will always be thankful they were not only adopted, but adopted together, into a loving forever home. Even though Lollie should be thanking Dyson for hugging her at the right time as a little pup, she can't stop tormenting him. It's the big sister thing to do.

CREATING A RESCUE DOG

"Saving one dog will not change the world, but surely for that one dog, the world will change forever."
~Karen Davison~

Dogs are the most amazing animals on the planet, and I challenge you to prove me wrong. They show us how incredible they are every day by bringing solace to lonely people; providing comfort to the elderly; defending our borders; fighting side by side with our military on foreign lands; doling out emotional aid for abused children; bringing independence to the disabled; and many other life-altering actions. Dogs unselfishly offer many services that enrich our society, and they ask for nothing in return; absolutely nothing. They obey, love, trust, accept, embrace, worship, entertain, and adore us. At the very least, we should help them when they find themselves homeless, neglected, or injured.

I believe rescue dogs are not damaged. Dogs arrive at rescue organizations through no fault of their own, and their rescue journey can take many different avenues.

First and foremost, if a pet owner needs to surrender a dog, they must contact a rescue organization to begin the surrendering process. If the organization has space available, they will ask the dog owner to sign an official surrender form. The document will inform the rescue what type of foster home or shelter placement would be best for the dog. It is also a legal document, so the owner understands the rescue takes ownership of the dog. Often, the owner will need to relinquish all medical records for the dog. They may be required to sign a Letter of Release with their veterinary clinic.

Surrendering a dog to a rescue organization is not as easy as ripping off a Band-Aid. Each rescue organization will have policies and procedures that must be adhered to during the surrender process. The main objective is to ensure the dog has an easy transition. Most importantly, a unique foster home or space in a shelter must be available to match the dog's needs. Surrendering a dog is a process, not an event.

PERSONAL HOME SURRENDERS

Some rescue dogs have been dearly loved and have already been part of a supportive family. Sometimes these families are faced with the fact they can no longer care for the dog because of financial or economic hardship, a child's birth, allergies, divorce, or personal illness. Circumstances like these force the owner to make the agonizing, heartbreaking decision to surrender a dog to rescue. These families and individuals love their dogs, but they understand they must make the painful decision to offer the opportunity of a new home so their dog can live a happy and fulfilled life with another owner. And no one should be ashamed when they need to surrender a dog. It is a complex and highly emotional decision to make.

The hard reality is some pet/owner relationships don't work out. Both the owner and the dog should be happy with the relationship, and the owner should never feel they don't have options when things are not working.

SURRENDERS FROM DREADFUL HOMES

Sadly, some dog owners are neglectful or abusive towards their pets. The best-case scenario is when these owners voluntarily surrender the dog to a rescue organization. In other cases, law enforcement officials may be forced to seize the dog after an extensive investigation. Police may need to remove a dog during a drug or weapons raid. Local officials may have taken a dog away while investigating animal cruelty, hoarding, or negligence cases. If a dog is a victim of abuse or other devastating circumstances, an extraordinary rescue or shelter will work with the dog to rebuild its confidence and trust.

When a previously abused dog arrives at a rescue, the organization rarely has a complete picture of the dog's past. These dogs will often stay in foster care or at a shelter for as long as it takes them to decompress and let their personalities shine. If the dog requires physical or emotional assistance, it will receive immediate veterinary medical care or behavioral training.

LOST DOGS

Animal control authorities often encounter lost dogs, and occasionally they may be unsuccessful in finding the owners. These dogs are held at a shelter for a mandated amount of time before being made available for adoption. Of course, microchipped dogs or dogs wearing ID tags with up-to-date owner information will make their way home safely. But if volunteers cannot locate the owners, they will help the dog find a loving forever home.

In the past, society viewed lost dogs as strays, but now they see them as needing help. With the creation of abandoned dog sites on Facebook, Instagram, and other social media platforms, there is plenty of support for reuniting dogs with their owners. It's a win for everyone as it results in faster reunions and keeps dogs out of shelters and rescues, freeing up space for homeless or surrendered dogs.

ABANDONED DOGS

Many cruel people abandon their dogs in rural areas on the road or leave them in the woods. There is no reason to abandon a dog with so many rescue organizations available to help, but unfortunately, it still happens. Some owners may dump the dog because they no longer want it, or the dog is too old to hunt or breed. Some people even leave their dogs behind in houses and apartments when they move out. Families that have suffered eviction notices may feel they have no other option but to leave the dog behind. Hopefully, someone finds the dog and calls animal control or local shelters to help provide the dog with a safe environment. Most jurisdictions have enacted laws to protect dogs from being abandoned or left behind in empty homes.

EUTHANASIA

Some dog owners take their dog to their veterinarian to be euthanized when they no longer want it, can no longer care for it, or when they feel the dog is too old and they want a younger dog. If a compassionate veterinarian feels the dog could still have many happy and healthy years to live, they may speak to the owner about surrendering the dog to a rescue. Most veterinary clinics have an intimate relationship with local rescue groups, so the clinic can ask the family to sign an official surrender document after explaining the rescue options available. Veterinarians are in the business of saving animals' lives.

I do not know of any veterinarians who will euthanize a healthy, happy dog because a family has grown tired of it. Unethical breeders often take their older breeding dogs to be euthanized when they can no longer generate income. Again, a veterinarian will usually explain other options available to the breeder and contact a rescue organization.

DEATH OF A DOG'S OWNER

Dogs can also arrive at rescue organizations when an owner unexpectedly passes away. If the surviving family members cannot care for the dog, they may surrender it to a rescue organization. Abandoning a dog after the death of a relative frequently happens if the owner has not made arrangements for their dog in their legal will. Remember Leona Helmsley and the fortune she left to her dog? You do not have to do the same, but preparations should be made for your dog just as you would for your children.

Arrangements can be as simple as having a conversation with a family member or close friend, in which you can ask if they would agree to take in your pet if something ever happened to you. Some people will leave the designated person some money to help with the future costs associated with the dog. It's that easy to ensure your best friend is taken care of should something happen to you.

DIVORCE

At times dogs are relinquished to a rescue organization after a marital breakdown. Neither of the partners may be able to take on the responsibility for the dog as a single person. The former partners may be moving to different apartments or condominiums that do not allow dogs or have restrictive size requirements. If the divorce is acrimonious, joint custody of the dog may be impossible.

INTERNATIONAL DOGS

Some rescue dogs make their way to North America from foreign lands. Dogs such as Galgos and Podencos from Spain are flown to North America to find permanent homes. Both breeds are used for hunting in Spain and are abandoned after the hunting season ends.

War-torn countries such as Ukraine, Afghanistan, or Syria have worked with volunteers at international rescue organizations to safely fly dogs to North America to find loving forever homes.

Street dogs or free-range dogs can also make their way to North America to be adopted. These dogs may come from countries such as Mexico, India, or Morocco, to name a few.

ANIMAL TESTING

Dogs can arrive at rescue organizations from animal testing labs across North America. A laboratory may surrender them voluntarily or the dogs may be seized after an investigation. When it comes to dogs being used in animal testing, beagles seem to be the most often used breed of dog.

ANIMAL HOARDING

Hoarding animals is a complicated and highly emotional issue, and people are far too quick to pass judgment. Rarely are animal hoarding situations actual intentional animal abuse cases, but amassing animals is common. Most hoarding incidents begin innocently and naively by a person taking in a few stray dogs. The person may feel they are providing a homeless dog with a safe environment. However, when multiple strays are involved, they begin to breed if the dogs are not spayed or neutered. The situation snowballs and becomes overwhelming for the owner, both emotionally and financially.

Most hoarding situations occur when lonely older adults experience separation from their family and community. Some individuals may have mental health issues, so they may not be aware of the stressful situation unfolding in their homes. But animal advocates agree; animal hoarding is particularly heartbreaking for the animals caught in these unfortunate circumstances.

You may not be aware of a hoarding situation in your community. A few things to look for include visibly dirty windows, foul smells emanating from the house, a homeowner who cannot confidently say how many animals live in the house, or the animals you can see from the street appear stressed or unclean.

If you are aware of a hoarding situation, you can offer help, or alert local authorities. Animal control officers can assist in removing the dogs and rescue organizations will find homes for the dogs and they may offer support for the individual. The officers often reach out to private rescue organizations to help find foster homes for the dogs. Some of these dogs may be stressed or unsocialized, but a skilled trainer can often help the dogs overcome the trauma.

DOGFIGHTING

As upsetting as it is for me to type these words, dogfighting happens all over North America. I will never understand how people can use a loving, social creature for deadly acts of human entertainment. Sadly, pit bulls seem to be the most popular breed used in dogfights, but this is most likely because the breed is known to be people pleasers. When the Michael Vick (former quarterback in the National Football League) fighting dogs were discovered, a friend told me, it was one of the first times the public viewed pit bulls as victims instead of offenders.

I have spoken to law enforcement officers, animal control officers, and lawyers many times about dogfighting. The one thing they all agree on: it is difficult and dangerous to infiltrate a dogfighting ring, and even more challenging to break one up.

Former fighting dogs may make their way into rescue organizations from time to time. It's reasonable to assume that the fighting dogs came from animal seizures or were found wandering, as many people involved in organizing dogfights, abandon the dogs.

A few years ago, a married couple found a dog in their front yard. The dog had a chain around her neck, but they did not know she was a fighting dog. They took her to a veterinarian as she had many wounds over her thin body. The veterinarian told the couple the dog was most likely a bait dog for dogfighting. A bait dog is used as practice for fighting dogs. The family decided to keep her as a family pet. She had no issues other than being petrified when she was outside after dark.

When these dogs arrive at a rescue organization, they are temperament-tested and lovingly cared for. They are given every opportunity to overcome their abusive past so they can evolve into loving family pets.

FREE TO GOOD HOME

People involved in animal rescue often find troubling advertisements or postings on Social Media platforms offering *"Free Dog to Good Home."* This is never good news, for many reasons. If possible, volunteers will reach out and offer to pick up the dog immediately because the threat to euthanize the dog usually follows the posting.

If the *"Free to Good Home"* dogs land in the wrong hands, they may be used for breeding, bait dogs for dogfighting, or they may be abused by unsavory individuals. The dog may also be given to an inappropriate home, such as a home with kids, which the dog may not like children. Volunteers will place the dog with a trusted foster home and allow the dog to settle to let its personality shine. In time, they will find the dog a loving forever home.

SLED DOGS

The ugly truth is that sled dogs live a terrible life, and many pay for that lifestyle with their lives. Fern Levitt wrote and directed a documentary entitled *Sled Dogs*. It exposed the horrible living conditions of sled dogs and shed much-needed light on the dog sledding industry.

In 2010, a sled dog massacre occurred in British Columbia, Canada. A mushing company claimed their business was substantially down after the Winter Olympics, so they brutally slaughtered the dogs and buried them in a pit. They did not take the dogs to a veterinary clinic to be humanely euthanized, nor did they reach out to rescue organizations to help re-home them.

Retired, seized, or rescued sled dogs make wonderful pets. Their exercise needs are not as high as you would think. They do not need to run for hours at a time, and most would appreciate a couch to lounge on instead.

MEAT DOGS

Meat dogs are often rescued from rural areas outside North America and mainly from Asia. The dogs are raised or farmed for human consumption, but some may have been stolen from private homes or picked up from the streets. With time and hard work by animal advocates, many cultures appear to be turning away from the ancient tradition of eating dog meat, but there are still hotspots in various regions worldwide. Humane Society International continues to educate in certain areas around the globe, and of course, continues to rescue the dogs.

These dogs are highly stressed when they are rescued. Most have lived in small, cramped cages with multiple dogs crammed into the same cage. The cages are so small the dogs cannot stand up. The rescue organizations work with the dogs to help them overcome the trauma and stress, and to be adopted.

Eating dog meat never became mainstream, but it was controversial. Western society has made many racist comments about the ancient Korean tradition, which TV host Jay Leno was sued over. After a class-action lawsuit, he made an apology in 2021 for his decades of racist jokes about Koreans eating dog meat.

CRUELTY SEIZURES

One of the most challenging things to witness is cruelty seizures. Cruelty seizures happen after authorities have done a thoroughly inspected investigation. The seizures come from many sources, such as large or small-scale breeding facilities, cruelty cases, dogs tied outside with no protection from the elements, and claims of abuse or negligence.

These dogs are taken for veterinarian welfare assessments and treated, if required. The dogs are documented and brought to foster care or a shelter. Depending on the seizure volume (number of dogs), a separate building may need to be temporarily rented and staffed.

BREED SPECIFIC LEGISLATION

Breed Specific Legislation (BSL) is a legal attempt to ban certain breeds of dogs solely based on how the dog looks. The legislation is based on myths, not facts. It often attempts to ban breeds like pit bulls, Rottweilers, or certain mixed-breed dogs from specific neighborhoods or cities. These dogs rarely have behavioral issues, yet the breed is banned. When the legislation becomes law, innocent dogs are often surrendered to rescues and shelters. The legislation is incredibly tough on families, shelters, rescues, and dogs.

HOMEWORK NOT DONE

Talk to any person operating a rescue organization. They will tell you that if people did proper research on the breed (or about dogs in general) beforehand, the dog owner would not be surrendering their dog. Some of the comments rescue organizations and shelters hear are: the dog grew too big (Great Pyrenees, Rottweiler, Newfoundland, Bernese Mountain); it sheds too much (any dog); it's too much work (any dog); or housetraining is too hard.

Before bringing a dog into your home, you must research the breed or breed mix. Consider how much time you have to commit to training the dog and how much time you will be able to spend with the dog. Research into the dog's size, energy, and breed traits is always helpful. A little homework will eliminate potential heartache for the family, including the children and the surrendered dog.

BLACK DOG SYNDROME

Unbelievably, black dogs tend to be surrendered more often and are usually the last to get adopted. The syndrome is also fed by the fact that black dogs don't photograph well, so people can't see their faces or read their emotions. Therefore, black dogs are often overlooked.

I feel the entertainment industry, including social media, has contributed to this phenomenon. They tend to portray large black dogs such as Rottweilers or Dobermans as villains, contributing to the stigma. The phenomenon is evident in most television shows and movie studios. It does not help that most diabolical characters also wear black clothing.

My husband and I owned two boisterous male Labrador Retrievers at one time; a yellow and a black. One afternoon after I returned from taking them for a walk, a dear friend called me. She had driven past me with her five-year-old son. As they passed, her son asked, "Do you think the yellow dog is good and the black dog is bad?" She knew both dogs behaved well and wasn't sure how to answer her son. I explained the black dog syndrome to her.

AN INCIDENT

Often, when families try to surrender a dog, they use the excuse that the dog bit someone, when in fact the incident did not happen. Most dogs go through life without biting a human or another dog. If, in fact, a bite did happen, a responsible rescue organization will investigate the circumstances of why the dog bit. Did the dog feel threatened? Why was the child left unsupervised with a dog? Did the child have food? Is the dog not socialized, was it abused, or was it tied permanently outside?

Most dogs will only bite when they feel threatened, startled, or scared. They may bite because they are protecting something of high value to them. If a responsible organization takes in a dog with a bite history, they will hire a trainer to help the dog move forward. A responsible organization will also make the adopter aware of the reasons and circumstances of the bite. First and foremost, organizations always strive to keep the public safe, no matter the cost.

DOG OWNER RELOCATIONS

Some people may feel their dog is too old to move far away. They may think that putting their dog on a long international flight will be unsafe for elderly or even younger dogs. There may be long quarantine requirements for dogs going to new countries. Some families may feel the quarantine restrictions are too harsh for their dog. These families will contact rescues and shelters to have the dog rehomed.

Renters or condominium owners may also discover that they are either not allowed to have dogs or their dog is over the allowable size after they have moved in. In desperation, they too will contact organizations to help rehome the dog.

Sadly, some families or individuals may not want to bother moving their dogs, so they end up at a shelter or rescue.

PRONG, SHOCK, AND CHOKE COLLAR

Dogs that have been trained with painful punishment-inducing collars can often end up in rescues. The dogs may exhibit as fearful and nervous, as they do not trust humans. Dogs trained with these detrimental instruments can and do suffer psychologically. Some can recover from the abuse with a certified trained who uses positive reinforcement training methods. Many rescue organizations will not adopt out a dog to an individual who uses prong, shock, or choke collars. These same rescues may have a clause included in the adoption contract that clearly states adopters cannot use these collars on dogs from the organization, including the use of electric containment fencing. Many countries such as Norway, Sweden, and Austria have instituted a ban on abusive collars, making it illegal to sell/buy or use one on a dog. Petco, a large pet retailer, has stopped carrying electronic collars.

I have a friend who is a dog trainer. If a client arrives with a dog wearing a prong collar, he offers them a better, kinder collar to use. He also saves the prong collars for me, which I turn into jewelry and give away as educational pieces.

If you are currently using a prong, shock or choke collar, please consider other painless options for your dog. You may be using these collars and you may not be aware how detrimental they are to your dog's mental and physical health. An uninformed dog trainer or retail pet supply store may have sold it to you without understanding the pain and damage it inflicts. Maya Angelou said it best, "Do the best you can until you know better. Then when you know better, do better."

CHAINED DOGS

Being tethered or chained outside permanently is a terrible way for a dog to live. Even though many jurisdictions have legislative laws regarding the length of time a dog can be tied out, the rules are often violated. A social animal like a dog should never live this kind of life. Many can struggle, even after they have been cut loose and rescued. They may suffer from aggression towards people or other dogs. They may become food aggressive or fearful of indoor life. A rescue organization will always work closely with these dogs to help them move forward from the trauma.

To put the life of a chained dog into perspective, imagine living in your attic. Your family and friends are living their life in your house. They celebrate holidays, anniversaries, birthdays, and they have impromptu parties. You can hear them, smell the food, and listen to the music, but you cannot participate. That is the life of a chained dog.

I remember a tied-out dog that made his way to a wonderful rescue organization because people kept reporting his horrible life to the authorities. He was filthy, covered in mats, his water bowl was frozen or empty, and he was not fed regularly. People in the neighborhood were sneaking food to the dog late at night, and they also witnessed his family do the unthinkable. They put a fence around their backyard but moved the dog to the other side of the wall so they wouldn't have to look at him.

A volunteer from a responsible rescue organization knocked on their door and asked if they may consider surrendering the dog to the rescue organization. The man told them to take the dog away because he was going to take it to the woods and shoot it. The dog ended up living a wonderful life with a loving family.

THE LAST SURRENDERED DOG I PICKED UP

Dogs have rightfully earned a coveted spot in our society, and they deserve to be protected. They should be in loving homes surrounded by supportive people who love them and consider them family members.

Many terrific, friendly dogs are looking for loving homes, and they come from many different backgrounds. They are waiting at rescues and shelters, and they come in every size, weight, age, personality, sex, or breed/mixed breed you could desire. We owe them an opportunity to become cherished family members in homes where they can thrive.

I have picked up many family-surrendered dogs over the years, and I was happy to deliver them to a safe, experienced foster home. It meant I was moving them from a bad situation to a protected temporary home. But after quite a few years of doing this, I became tormented. It became a never-ending parade of unwanted, unloved, emotionally broken, confused, depressed dogs sitting in my backseat, and they came from every walk of life. I picked up dogs from million-dollar homes, apartments, and low-income housing, and I even agreed to meet people in public parking lots. Of course, the surrendering households had previously signed legal documents to hand the dog over to the rescue organization.

The last surrendered dog I picked up just about crushed me, and I knew I had to stop before I burned out. The previous owners were negligent, and the poor dog had psychologically shut down. She would not make eye contact with me, and she shivered so severely I thought she might have a heart attack. The owner practically threw the dog into my arms and yelled, "She's your @&#£% problem now." As he walked away, I thought, at least he surrendered the dog to an outstanding rescue organization, because many don't make it. They are tossed in the street, abandoned in a forest, or killed.

I found out much later that they had bought her from a Kijiji advertisement to breed her so they could sell the offspring. She lived in a cage in his kitchen for two years, so she was never properly socialized or loved. Luckily, she never produced a litter to sell.

I gently carried the little beagle-mix to my car and placed her in the backseat. This little dog came without a collar, bedding, bowls, food, or toys. I then drove her to the foster family's home. I waited with the foster family for over two hours, trying to gain this girl's trust so we could get her out of my car. When she finally slinked out of the car, she kept pancaking on the ground out of sheer fear. It took another hour to get her into their house, and it was only about a ten-foot walk.

My drive home was terrible. I kept having to pull over because I was in tears and emotionally spent. When my husband saw me pull into our laneway, he promptly poured me a glass of wine and placed a box of Kleenex on the table.

The foster parents sent me many pictures of the dog in the coming days and weeks. The images showed me how well she was doing. She had blossomed into a funny, confident girl, and the foster parents had fallen in love with her. They decided to make her an official family member and adopted her. This term is lovingly referred to as a "foster-fail" in the rescue world.

COMPASSION FATIGUE

The sad truth is that burnout is incredibly high for individuals involved in animal rescue. I recognized some of the signs, and I took action to protect myself. My symptoms included feeling overwhelmed, not sleeping, and feeling as if I was spread too thin. It's a delicate balancing act to ensure your personal life is happy, your career doesn't suffer, and you're continuing your rescue endeavors.

The first thing I learned was to say no, and that step alone helped my well-being. I stopped picking up surrendered dogs, but I did continue driving foster dogs to veterinary appointments. It was the smartest thing I did to ensure I could continue my advocacy work to support homeless dogs. Animal rescuers are not superheroes. We don't wear capes or have superpowers. We are real people simply trying to help man's best friend when he needs assistance.

I have always found rescue dogs to be forgiving, resilient, and downright inspirational. They tend to figure out quite quickly that their new home is a safe environment. The dogs only need to be given a chance with ample time to settle into their new surroundings and routine.

If you're looking for a positive experience that will open your heart and enrich your soul, adopt a homeless rescue dog. Watching that dog thrive and flourish in your home will be one of the most positive, life-altering experiences of your life. You will truly feel, every day, as if you've hit the jackpot. Even Las Vegas can't guarantee those odds.

"You can't buy love, but you can rescue it."
~unknown~

EDDIE

"The only place a dog should race is into your arms, for a long embrace."
~unknown~

After retiring from a lackluster but comical career on the racetrack, Eddie found himself rehomed. He lacked the prey instinct required to be a successful racer. If the track owners had been innovative and replaced the fake bunny with a McDonald's cheeseburger, Eddie would have made them millions.

His adoptive family firmly believes he may have been the worst racer ever to exist because this handsome boy is a couch potato, through and through. He does not need beauty rest, but he successfully fulfills his daily sofa time quota. He lovingly gazes out the window wishing it was Saturday night, not because he wants to party, but because he loves his weekend pizzas.

This boy does not have proper foodie training or a three-star chef's taste for food, but his favorite foods will surprise everyone. He loves cooked potatoes, peanut butter, bananas, bread, and we already mentioned his love affair with pizza. From time to time, his parents will make him what they hilariously refer to as The Elvis Sandwich: a peanut butter and banana sandwich. One sideways glance from Eddie, and you, too, will be handing over all your peanut butter and running to the store to buy him bananas.

Eddie's love of potatoes means he will turn himself inside out for one when his family is having a big weekend breakfast with home fries. His father will hide one in his closed hand, and Eddie has to hit the right hand before he can have the coveted potato. Afterwards, his dad has to act like a blackjack dealer in Las Vegas, waving his open hands to prove he doesn't have another hidden potato.

Eddie can be forgiven for his lowbrow taste in food because he's the best-behaved dog ever. He's sweet, and affectionate, and loves every person or dog he meets. He affectionately and generously shares his couch with every two-legged or four-legged soul in the universe, but don't ask him to share his pizza—we all have limits.

Eddie's family devoted quite a bit of time and research to finding the perfect dog for their clan. His adoptive mom had experience with a greyhound, so they reached out to a local rescue organization. The group they contacted had over thirty years of experience rehoming this majestic breed, so they felt they would be in good hands, or maybe even good paws. The family eagerly filled out an application and were accepted to attend a four-hour orientation session. There were no dogs at the presentation, just other potential adopters looking to provide a wonderful forever home for the same breed.

It was a well-rounded, defined process to adopt from this organization, which impressed the family. After the presentation, the association booked a home visit, and they brought a greyhound along for the trip. Next, they secured a time to meet a dog that matched all the doggy personality traits they had requested. The family specifically asked for a "velcro-dog" who was social with both people and other dogs. The group's president recommended a dog named Ed Sheeran. Yes, Eddie was named after a famous singer.

The family of three fell in love with Eddie's fawn color, doe-like eyes, and wonderfully open and relaxed disposition. The family of three became a joyful family of four.

Eddie loves his entire family, but he has an extraordinary relationship with his handsome teenage brother, Liam. Liam looks after all of Eddie's needs, and when he is not at school, they spend their time together on their shared loveseat. Liam is a wonderful young man with a gentle animal-loving soul.

Eddie's family was musically inclined long before Eddie entered their life, but that has changed. Quite by accident, Eddie's family discovered that he loves to sing loudly, and he hits all the octaves, just like his namesake, Ed Sheeran. Eddie especially loves to sing along to The Beatles, Radiohead or, wait for it, Scottish bagpipes. Maybe Eddie is Ed Sheeran, wearing a dog suit. You never know.

Most, if not all, pet parents will do anything humanly possible for their dog, and Eddie's are no exception. Eddie had a simple surgery at his veterinary clinic one afternoon, but there were complications. His parents had to race him to an emergency clinic for a frantic lifesaving blood transfusion. This blood transfusion involved two live dog donations from two different rescue dogs, one being my dog, Sheena. Dogs in the blood donation program are pre-screened and pre-approved for the medical procedure.

The emergency clinic called me a few days later; Eddie's family was on the phone. They wanted to thank me because my best friend saved their best friend. In tears, I implored them to give the family all my contact information. I got together with Eddie's family, and to my surprise, they gave me an emotion-filled handwritten card, a bottle of wine, and a gift card to buy something for my dog. They did the same for the other donor dog. If that doesn't melt your heart, nothing in this world ever will. Eddie has the absolute best family he could have wished for, and he lets them know by belting out a tune from time to time and sharing his pizza.

MUMFORD

"Most of us have been told that angels have wings.
But some of us have learned that they have paws."
~unknown~

This handsome rescue boy, Mumford, was abandoned in a box in the woods with his two littermates when he was only weeks old. Luckily the authorities were contacted, and all three pups made their way safely to a rescue organization and were eventually adopted.

A young, hard-working couple adopted Mumford; his dad is in construction and his mom works in healthcare. Both parents agree that Mumford was a great addition to the family. He's an animated boy who entertains his parents from the moment he gets up in the morning until he sleeps at night. He's a husky mix with a beautiful thick coat you can lose your hands in. Mumford is now eight years old, but his parents say he still acts like a puppy.

When Mumford lost his baby teeth, one adult tooth did not come in. He also lost one of his top back molars when he cracked it. Missing two teeth does not slow him down when he's eating, but he looks like a retired hockey player, but more handsome than Wayne Gretzky.

Mumford jumps out of his parents' bed at 5:30 am seven days a week because he wants his breakfast NOW. If his parents don't move fast enough, he helps them along. He also expects his dinner at 4:00 pm sharp, and his parents know they mustn't be late because there will be (comical) consequences.

When Mumford has finished his dinner, he grabs one of two toys: a stuffed red Angry Bird or a little, worse-for-wear, stuffed lion he has had since he was a puppy. Once his toy is selected, he turns on his classic Husky-whining voice and runs through the house. This does not stop until he has hidden the toy either in one of the beds or between the couch cushions. He then un-makes his parents bed, every night. You could say Mumford offers turndown service just like a high-end hotel.

Mumford has a long list of hilariously silly quirks. He loves to rub his face along the couch, then shove his sweet head between the cushions as if no one can see him. When his mom has finished her shower and has wrapped her hair in a towel, Mumford will grab the towel, take it to her bed and then lay on his back, rubbing the towel on the bedspread.

He loves to go for car rides, but he insists on sitting in the backseat, passenger side, and the window must be open for his sweet little head. He must also have a dish full of water on every drive. A boy has to stay hydrated. He loves going to the vet, but it's challenging to weigh him as his butt is too wiggly on the scale.

Mumford also loves going to the beach, and his mom knows all too well what happens as soon as his feet hit the sand or water: he does a number two, without fail. Why, you ask? No one knows but Mumford, and he's not going to share that secret anytime soon. He adores the outdoors so much, he loves to go camping, but he hates bugs, so his grandmother bought him a screen tent to enjoy the outdoors without becoming mosquito bait.

Mumford adores his two rescue cat siblings. He follows them everywhere and gently nudges them with his nose when he wants to play. It's not abnormal for his mom to come home and find both cats comfortable in a sunbeam on the kitchen table, with Mumford right beside them.

CREATING A RESCUE DOG

Anyone who works in an office will tell you: no one likes paperwork, but Mumford has taken that dislike to a new level. If there is a paper towel, toilet paper, tissues, or napkins within his reach, he will shred them into a million tiny pieces. Again, no one knows why; it's just the beauty of being Mumford.

His parents cannot put the grocery bags on the floor, not because they may contain paper items, but because Mumford will search through the bags and drag out the lettuce, his favorite food. He also likes blueberries and strawberries, but lettuce is at the top of his list. His mom makes homemade frozen yogurt treats for him. She adds peanut butter or fruit into the frozen cubes, and she frequently finds Mumford sitting in front of the freezer, patiently waiting for one. Hopefully she doesn't add lettuce to the frozen cubes, or Mumford may never leave the house again.

When his parents eat their dinner, Mumford will sit in front of them, ensuring they finish their vegetables. His dad usually ends first, which immediately makes Mumford turn invisible. He will drag himself along the floor on his belly, slip up onto his mom's seat, and slink across her lap. Of course, being an eighty-pound dog, she doesn't notice him.

He sleeps between his parents every night, but he has one last ritual before bedtime. When his mom has finished brushing her teeth, Mumford must go outside for one last breath of nighttime air and take a look at the stars. This procedure must be followed, or no one gets to go to bed.

Mumford is a sweet, well-loved boy who is a valued member of a wonderful family. If you ever get a chance to meet him, bring a head of lettuce. You'll be his friend for life.

DAISY

"Some things just fill your heart, without trying"
~unknown~

Daisy's parents describe her as loyal, goofy, and present. They said she has a sense of humor that keeps them in stitches and that Daisy is deeply loved.

Daisy had a traumatic start in life, and some of her history remains a mystery. Her previous owner heartlessly left her tied to a pole downtown on a scorching summer day without access to water. The authorities were contacted, and they claimed the nameless abandoned dog.

A young man decided to go to the shelter after Daisy was picked up. He wanted to look at the dogs because he was considering adoption. While at the shelter, the staff told him about Daisy. He instantly fell in love with her soulful face and sweet disposition. He happily adopted her, but the municipality soon elected Breed Specific Legislation (BSL). The legislation came with punishing and punitive penalties against breeds such as her. BSL punishes a dog for how it looks, not because that dog did anything wrong. It's an outdated, antiquated law that makes dogs and loving owners suffer.

The young man frantically called his parents on the other side of the country because he worried about Daisy's safety and well-being. They instructed their son to jump on a plane with Daisy and bring her home. He did just that, and Daisy never looked back.

Daisy lives in the lap of luxury on a one-acre country estate. The property is fully fenced, so Daisy can run safely for as long and as hard as she wants. She goes for dreamy beach walks along the Pacific Ocean with her parents, and she also enjoys a group dog nature walk in the woods with a motley crew of canines. When Daisy is on the group walk, she hilariously mothers all the dogs and leads the pack during the adventure.

This sweet girl is obsessed with babies and young children. She smothers them with kisses and is exceptionally gentle and loving with the squirmy children. She is a beautiful dog who is devoted and loyal to those that enter her life.

Daisy may have been about six years old when she was adopted, making her twelve or thirteen years old now. Even though she has lost her hearing, she is whip-smart and has learned hand signals. Her parents agree she may have learned to read lips because they can communicate with her as if she can still hear. They say that looking into her eyes, they see an old sensitive soul. As much as she loves her parents, she is her mom's shadow and follows her everywhere.

When Daisy goes to her veterinary clinic, she gets the bulk of attention whenever she has an appointment. The staff and veterinarians fawn over her and lavish her with treats and loads of belly rubs. Daisy loves the attention—unsurprising, seeing what life was like before she was adopted.

Poor Daisy had been bred to exhaustion before she was found abandoned, tethered to a pole many years ago. And even though her loving family has recently been given a grim medical diagnosis, mostly because of the excessive breeding, they say their grounded, unique, incredible girl is doing very well.

Rescue dogs like Daisy usually, and quite quickly, figure out they are in a safe home. She's an easy breezy girl, and if you meet her on a Pacific Ocean beach, get ready for lots of kisses. Lavishing affection is Daisy's unique talent.

RUCKER

"Happiness doesn't result from what we get, but from what we give."
~Ben Carson~

Rucker is a rescue boy who also saves other dogs. He was adopted by a sweet family of four as a very young pup. He arrived at a local shelter with his three siblings, and his family doesn't know much about his past life. He may have been surrendered to the rescue organization, or he may have been part of a seizure. Either way, Rucker is happy his family picked him.

Rucker's mom hilariously said, "He is the laziest dog I have ever known, and he would sleep until noon every day if I let him." She works from home, and it isn't out of Rucker's character to put himself back to bed during the workday. He is very playful and super friendly with everyone he meets, except for ducks. He will chase ducks if he runs into one. Why? No one knows.

Therefore, his family keeps him on a leash when he's swimming, which he loves to do. Oh, Rucker!!!

Given that he's a super-friendly boy, he doesn't mind going to the vet and gets a kick out of the visit. His mom thinks he figures he's just "going to see the treat man." Speaking of treats, Rucker's all-time favorite treat is ice cubes. Yes, you heard that right. He loves them so much he will sit in front of the refrigerator waiting for one. If one of his staff doesn't come along to grab one for him, he will try to open the freezer drawer by himself. If only he'd help put the groceries away.

Outside of ice cubes, Rucker loves peanut butter, and if his sister should be eating peanut butter toast, he'll magically and quietly appear behind her. He also loves donuts and Starbucks pup-uccinos. He'll hang his head out the window in the drive-thru in anticipation of his special doggy coffee.

Rucker lives by one important rule: all stuffed toys must be dead when they enter his house. He doesn't just rip them open and de-stuff the toy; they must be left in small, microscopic pieces that no coroner from *Law & Order* could ever identify. That's the rule.

As stated before, Rucker is a loving boy, and he shares that love with his family. His bedtime routine is a mish-mash. Instead of sleeping exclusively with one family member, he'll sleep with his parents one night then alternate nights between the kids. Maybe he thinks he's Goldilocks from the children's book *Three Little Bears*, and he's just trying to figure out which bed is the softest. Anything is possible when it comes to Rucker.

After a good night's sleep, Rucker loves going to the dog park and playing fetch in his unique way. His mom will throw the ball as far as possible, and Rucker will return with it every time. But he drops it five feet in front of her, so she too has to retrieve the ball. He's a silly boy, but his family loves his quirks.

Speaking of quirks, he sits on a pillow when he knows he's about to be fed, and goodness knows what happens if his water bowl is empty. He flips and bangs the bowl all over the kitchen until it is filled up. He also insists the window in the backseat of the car must be down when he goes for a drive. He'll let out a little bark telling you to hit the down button if it's closed. Moreover, he figures out quite quickly where he's off to, and as soon as he sees the destination, he starts to pace in anticipation from the backseat. He's a smart, funny, and entertaining boy with a personality as large as his heart.

His heart is so big he is a member of the blood donor program at an emergency veterinary hospital. He's been a member for about three years, suggesting he may have helped save as many as ten best friends. He will happily continue in the lifesaving program for as long as possible because he loves giving back, and the clinic has the best treats ever.

Rucker is one lucky rescue dog, and he hopes all dogs waiting for loving homes find one just like his. He also hopes they follow his critical rule of life: all stuffed toys must be destroyed.

THE UGLY SIDE OF DOG BREEDING

"When a man's best friend is his dog, that dog has a problem."
~Edward Abbey~

Let me be clear; I despise the term "puppy mill." It's a fluff phrase. We should be calling the industry precisely what it is: mass dog farming for profit. Its sole purpose is to produce as much product as possible while keeping expenses low to protect its revenue stream.

The same can be said about backyard breeders (BYB), as they also breed strictly for profit. Both types of breeding operation have little regard for the health of the breeding dogs or the litters of puppies they manufacture. Sadly, dog breeding produces vast amounts of easy money for operators, with little governance or oversight. This chapter will uncover and expose questionable breeding practices.

MASS DOG FARMING

Large-scale dog breeding businesses are characterized by enormous breeding facilities with deplorable living conditions, and the operators show absolutely no concern for the welfare of the dogs. Often these dogs are stuck in cages stacked on top of each other. The dogs live in filth from feces and urine twenty-four hours a day and are not fed regularly, resulting in malnourishment. They are repeatedly yelled at if they bark or whine. Many of these facilities keep electric shock collars on the breeding dogs to control the noise. The dogs are not socialized, and in many cases they never see the light of day. They receive little or no veterinary care, and most times, the public is not provided with an opportunity to visit the facility. The worst part of the business model is the continuous confinement of the dogs and the lack of human interaction.

Often these breeding warehouses cannot produce paperwork for proof of genealogy or offer health guarantees. They also refuse to take back a dog if you can no longer care for your pet. A responsible breeder will take on a lifetime responsibility for the dogs they produce. They do not want their dogs to end up at a rescue organization or be euthanized. Mass dog farmers do not care about the welfare of the dogs they produce or the risk of diseases they can inherit or are born with, such as periodontal disease, ear infections, eye disorders, parvovirus, giardia and many other parasites or infections.

Many people have seen the videos and photos taken by investigators during and after a facility's dogs have been seized. This evidence shows crates filled with petrified dogs stacked on top of each other. Usually, mould and mildew cover the walls. Ceilings will be shown as falling apart, as they are soaked with urine from the floor above. Authorities are shown wearing masks as the smell from urine and excrement can burn their eyes and lungs. The conditions are always inhumane and wretched for those poor dogs.

Puppies that should be chasing butterflies and falling over themselves are usually trapped in cramped cages and crates. Some may be throwing up or are lethargic, with their heads leaning on the crate walls. The images are always haunting.

The Humane Society of the United States (humanesociety.org) publishes an annual list entitled: "Horrible Hundred." It documents one hundred puppy mills in the USA that sell their dogs through pet stores or online. Many of the businesses are repeat animal abuse offenders, and sadly, many are registered as American Kennel Club (AKC) breeders. Surprisingly, the AKC conducts very few breeding facility inspections to hold many of their members accountable for their breeding practices. In 2013, the Humane Society estimated 10,000 puppy mills were operating across the United States, with an estimated 1,000 mills in Canada.

THE UGLY SIDE OF DOG BREEDING

BACKYARD BREEDERS (BYB)

Dogs produced by BYBs fare no better and are subject to the same conditions as dogs from large-scale breeding facilities. These smaller-scale breeding facilities are just as damaging to a dog's health and wellness as any large commercial breeding business. BYB operators may own one or a few female dogs and a male dog they use for breeding purposes. In the absence of a male dog, they may randomly use a neighbor's dog or advertise that they are looking for a stud dog on social media.

BYBs have little knowledge or experience with breeding standards and usually state their reasons for breeding as: just for fun; they wanted their kids to experience birth; she's such a great dog we wanted to share her personality with others; or they say it was an accidental pregnancy. Please make no mistake: BYBs are breeding their family pets to make money. They never take back a dog, and they offer no health guarantees.

GREED VS. HEALTH

Money made by both mass dog farmers and BYBs does not appear to be invested back into their respective businesses to enrich the breeding dogs' lives. The funds line the operator's pockets—greed wins over health.

They do not conduct health checks on the dogs or know their genealogy (line of descent traced from ancestors). They don't do genetic testing (checking for diseases or breed-specific conditions), and they often and knowingly turn out unhealthy dogs. Some of these irresponsible, cold-hearted breeders will sell the puppies before they are two months old and often kill the defective newborn pups, as they are not a source of revenue.

These are usually cash businesses, and the income is often unreported, so taxes are not paid. Money aside, the most significant issue is the unhealthy dogs they produce. The cost of caring for those dogs is a massive obligation transferred to the unsuspecting public who end up buying unhealthy pups.

Many of these dogs can be born with cleft palates, develop bone cancers at a young age, and suffer from chronic urinary tract infections. Some of these animals suffer from early blindness or deafness, experience hip dysplasia at young ages, have heart problems, exhibit lifelong aggression issues, and countless other life-threatening health conditions.

Many of these puppies can exhibit un-socialized behaviors. An extremely stressed mother dog (which includes most dogs living at mass dog farms or BYBs) can release hormones such as cortisol (also known as the fight-or-flight hormone) through the placenta to the unborn puppies. This transfer resets the hormonal balance of the unborn pup, adversely affecting the pup's development and can create skittish, nervous, anxious dogs as they mature, contributing to an agitated state for the rest of their lives. Therefore, poor breeding practices can lead to both unhealthy and antisocial dogs. It may be safe to say that not all bad dogs have bad owners. A small percentage may have poor genetics due to being poorly bred by unscrupulous breeders.

It's the age-old question of nature versus nurture. A problematic genetic background plays a huge role in the psychological development of dogs (nature). For example, I have friends who have owned their dogs since they were puppies. They are great dog owners who did the responsible thing with their dogs, such as puppy classes, maybe one or two levels of obedience, and they train their dogs with gentle reward-based training (nurture), yet their dogs struggle psychologically throughout their life.

Socializing your dog at an early age can help give your dog the tools to live a well-balanced life. However, poor breeding will negatively affect the dog's genetic blueprint. It would be best to buy a puppy or dog from a responsible, well-established breeder or a recognized responsible rescue organization.

Sadly, bad breeders survive because of the strong demand for dogs. Innocent buyers are often lied to regarding where the puppies were produced. It's challenging to monitor mass dog farms and BYBs, as these operations exist in isolated areas such as barns, dilapidated structures, private households, sheds, and basements throughout North America.

As challenging as it is to monitor these underground operations, there is only one way to end their practices; avoid buying their product. It doesn't mean you can't buy a puppy—you just have to verify the source from which you are buying and educate yourself about good breeding practices. If not, greed wins, and dogs will continue to suffer.

THE UGLY SIDE OF DOG BREEDING

GUARDIAN BREEDING CONTRACTS

Some breeders allow their breeding dogs or a puppy (eventually to be bred) to go to an approved home, but ownership of the dog belongs to the breeder. A Guardian Breeding Contract is signed between the household (guardian) and the breeder stipulating that the guardian agrees to allow the dog to be bred a certain number of times, over a limited number of years. The guardian provides a home for the dog; however, when the mating season begins, the dog is sent back to the breeder. A male breeding dog may stay with the breeder for a couple of weeks, but female dogs may be kept for several weeks or more.

The female dog may return to the breeder's facility before she whelps her puppies. She stays at the breeder's facility until the puppies are weaned. At that point, the dog returns to the guardian's home.

This type of breeding program promotes that a guardian provides a home for a dog where it can be loved and be part of a family. The breeders prey on the guardian's emotions, and they tout the benefits of not leaving the dog with the breeding establishment where it may not get the kind of care the guardian can provide.

The contract between the two parties should be closely scrutinized by the guardian before signing any agreement. The contract terms usually benefit the breeder more than the guardian and take advantage of potential dog owners who can't afford to buy a purebred animal from a breeder.

The contract may include how many times you must allow the dog to be bred. Maintenance and care are most likely downloaded to the guardian's home. It may also stipulate that the guardian has no ownership rights over any puppies produced. Many of these contracts include a clause that you must live within a certain distance from the breeder's home, limiting the guardian's freedom to move. Some breeders will demand a deposit from the guardian, which may or may not be returned after the mandated breeding commitment has been fulfilled. Other guardian contracts may include a harsh penalty, as high as USD $7,500.00, if the contract is not fulfilled.

Guardians are hoping to own a wonderful dog after allowing it to be bred for four or five years. While some contracts state the breeder is responsible for the cost of food, vaccinations and some veterinary care, it is a long road before the guardian has exclusive and legal ownership of the dog. Be very aware before entering such contracts with any breeder. Only the breeder is making money from the contract, accepting very little day-to-day responsibility for the bred dogs.

I feel, if a breeder cannot care for or offer loving attention to the dogs within the facility, they have too many breeding dogs. They may be running a mass dog farm.

SOCIAL MEDIA & PUPPY BROKERS

Nefarious breeders will create misleading websites on which to sell their dogs, and they also use social media platforms such as Facebook, Twitter, Instagram, and Kijiji. These sites showcase healthy puppies running on the grass, which is far from the truth. The breeding dogs are housed in filthy crates with their puppies. Many never see the light of day and have never had a kind hand caress their fur.

When you contact one of these breeders, they will discourage you from visiting their premises. They will try to frame it as doing you a favor and offer to meet you in a public parking lot. If you are not provided with an opportunity to meet the breeding dogs and observe the facility, you are most likely dealing with an illegitimate breeder or even a puppy broker. Yes, there is such a thing as a puppy broker. They exist because puppies are a hot commodity—like gold on the New York Stock Exchange.

Puppy brokers buy pups from unsavory breeders and resell them. The practice is not exclusive to North America. Puppy brokers are known to import planeloads of pups from all over the globe, and sadly, many of these pups die while in flight. These pups are often removed from the mother dog too early, and the dogs will suffer the consequences for the rest of their lives. A puppy needs to spend two to three months with its mother. She needs to nurse the pups and help socialize them to live a healthy, well-balanced life. But puppy brokers, BYBs, and large-scale breeders do not care because the breeding business is profitable for all parties involved, with little or no regulatory oversight.

THE UGLY SIDE OF DOG BREEDING

HOLLYWOOD, TRENDS, & DESIGNER DOGS

Unethical breeders benefit financially because of societal trends and demands for specific or popular breeds of the day. Movies can boost the demand for certain dog breeds. Hollywood movies such as *101 Dalmatians, Lassie Come Home, The Mask, Men in Black,* and *Turner & Hooch* increased the demand for the dog breeds featured in the stories. Breeders will often take advantage of this opportunity and start breeding the most popular dogs of the moment.

The demand for genetically altered dogs, better known as designer dogs, is strong. Designer breeders mate two different breeds to produce dogs they claim have the best features from each breed. These breeders may argue that the dogs they create are smaller than the standard recognized breed or require less grooming and maintenance. Some even claim to breed hypoallergenic dogs, but that trait is difficult to prove. Depending on the popularity of the designer dogs, they can be produced at both large-scale breeding facilities and BYBs, and then shipped throughout the world. I'm confident most people have heard about labradoodles (Labrador retriever and poodle mix).

Traditional registered kennel clubs define a purebred dog as a dog that has been selectively bred over many generations to breed true. When a dog breeds true, all the puppies produced will look alike and share the distinct breed traits. A few primary breed true standards include Labrador retrievers with solid-colored coats, Dalmatians with black spots, and Cocker Spaniels with wavy fur on their ears. Be aware of the traits you are looking for in a purebred dog and ensure that you are dealing with a trustworthy breeder, not a mixed-breed designer dog business.

Sadly, price does not deter buyers, with the cost usually significantly higher than for purebred dogs. Be aware if you purchase a dog from a mixed-breed business, as you may be buying a dog with minor or significant genetic defects. Breeding a large dog with a smaller breed dog can cause lifelong intolerable pain for that dog. Designer dogs such as Labradoodles (Labrador Retriever/Poodle), Golden Doodles (Golden Retriever/Poodle), or Puggle (Pug/Beagle) may grow to become incontinent, develop skin issues, or have many costly genetic health-related problems. Buyers should be aware of the risks involved when buying a designer dog. Buyer beware—you are not buying a purebred dog, and the price you pay should reflect that fact.

MENNONITE AND AMISH DOG FARMERS

It has been widely reported by credible media outlets that two different communities in North America, the Mennonites and the Amish, are actively involved in the dog breeding business. To be clear, not all Mennonite or Amish communities have dog farms, but sadly, many make plenty of money by breeding dogs.

The dogs are kept in crates or wire pens with little protection from the outdoor elements. Rescue organizations have discovered many of these dogs have been debarked, and many do not survive because of the deplorable living conditions.

Both communities have been reported as stating they believe dogs are livestock, just like cows or chickens. While both groups can make money from their livestock of cows and chickens by selling milk and eggs, dogs offer no economic benefits other than the puppies they produce. Therefore, the dogs are overbred with no regard for the dog's welfare. Having a social and domesticated animal live like livestock is disappointing. Given that dogs have unselfishly enriched humanity, they deserve better treatment.

KENNEL CLUBS

Registered kennel clubs promote purebred pedigreed dogs and the preservation of breed characteristics in those dogs. Dogs from a registered kennel club are supposed to have consistent traits, and the registered breeders are required to maintain the integrity of a specific breed. The breeder must also have the ability to show proof of lineage for the dogs they produce. Most of these breeders produce healthy, genetically sound, social dogs, but not all adhere to the standards.

I have four noteworthy issues with kennel clubs. My first issue is that I am against breeders who do not take back their dogs. Sadly, these dogs end up in shelters and rescues, or they may be euthanized when owners can no longer care for the dog. Some breeding contracts clearly state they will take back a dog, but the contract should also stipulate what happens to that dog if it is returned to the breeder.

THE UGLY SIDE OF DOG BREEDING

I believe it should be mandated in North America that if you breed dogs, you must have the capacity to take back the dogs that are produced in your facility and take responsibility for rehoming the dog. It's time for breeders to be held responsible for every dog they sell, which should be for the dog's lifetime. The breeder should report and provide evidence of rehoming to the kennel club consistently.

My second issue with most kennel clubs is the mutilation procedures performed on the dogs to conform to the kennel clubs' strict breed standards regarding what a specific breed should look like or resemble. The mutilation includes ear cropping, tail docking, dew claw removal, gluing ears shut and in some cases, debarking.

Ear cropping involves removing approximately two-thirds of the outer soft floppy part of the ear. The surgery includes re-setting the cartilage to make the ear erect. The dog must wear bandages and splints until the ears heal. This procedure causes considerable pain and discomfort to the dog.

Tail docking is the process of amputating the tail. Many breeds listed with kennel clubs must have their tails removed to meet specific breed standards, including but not limited to cocker spaniels and Rottweilers. In most cases, the tails are cut off by the breeder during the first weeks after the puppy is born. Some regions in North America have mandated that the surgery is to be performed exclusively by veterinarians. Some jurisdictions classify ear cropping and tail docking as cosmetic; therefore, they prohibit the procedure.

Breeders sometimes remove dew claws when the puppy is only days old. The dew claw is the thumb-like toe on a dog's front legs. In many cases, an anesthetic is not used for this procedure.

Many breeders of Airedale Terries, Welsh Terriers, or Wire Fox Terriers glue the puppy's ears shut at a young age for approximately three weeks to create a tip (triangle) shape of the ear. Some dogs may have to have it done twice, and some breeders even recommend removing the glue with scissors or shears. This practice can negatively affect the puppy's development and can be painful. Some dogs may incur dreadful ear infections while their ears are glued closed. Therefore, some breeders recommend you smell the ears daily to check for foul smells.

The American Kennel Club supports debarking. They claim on their website that "Debarking is a viable veterinary procedure that may allow a dog owner to keep a dog that barks excessively in its loving home rather than to be forced to surrender it to a shelter. Debarking should only be performed by a qualified, licensed veterinarian after other behavioral modification efforts to correct excessive barking have failed. As with other veterinary medical decisions, the decision to debark a dog is best left to individual owners and their veterinarians." Alexandra Horowitz, a New York Times bestseller author, summed up debarking in her book *Our Dogs, Ourselves*, as: "While many dog owners may find a barking dog annoying, surgery that removes part of or all of the vocal cords is like responding to a complaining, questioning, or scared child by stapling his mouth shut." Horowitz is a Senior Research Fellow and head of the Dog Cognition Lab at Barnard College, Columbia University. She is a widely respected leader and supporter of animal rights.

My third issue with kennel clubs is their support and promotion of dog shows, such as the National Dog Show by the Kennel Club of Philadelphia (presented by Purina), the AKC National Championship (presented by Royal Canin), the Westminster Dog Show (Westminster Kennel Club) and Crufts (The Kennel Club) in the United Kingdom.

It has been well documented that there is a significant increase in breeding for a specific breed after it has won the top spot at a dog show. It has also been well documented that BYBs and Mass Dog Farmers begin breeding the winning dog breed, strictly because of the financial opportunity created by the public's demand for the winning breed. Unfortunately, many of these breeds will end up in shelters and rescue organizations after the public's interest fades, the breed loses popularity, or the breed becomes overbred, creating unhealthy dogs.

My last issue with Kennel Clubs is their lack of support for rescue organizations.

THE UK KENNEL CLUB (THEKENNELCLUB.ORG.UK)

When writing this book (February 2022), I found a statement on their website under the tab "Find a Puppy or Rescue" regarding behavioral concerns with rescue dogs.

"Most rescue dogs have had at least one home and sometimes many homes. They can come with behavioural issues due to the fact they may have been rejected at least once and, in some cases, a number of times."

"Some will have been in kennels or a rescue centre for some considerable time. This will have an effect on dogs, especially those that are normally used to family life and constant attention. The dog may have been put in a rescue centre because of behavioural problems, which could include toileting indoors, excessive barking or destructive tendencies."

So, only rescue dogs have accidents inside, bark excessively, and are destructive? It's hypocritical for the UK Kennel Club to make such broad degrading statements about rescue dogs. Many of the same dogs they are making defamatory comments about may have come from a UK-registered Kennel Club.

THE AMERICAN KENNEL CLUB (AKC.ORG)

At this time, November 16, 2022, the AKC website has a tab at the bottom of the first page under "AKC Cares" titled "Rescue Network." You can find almost every breed in alphabetical order and click on that specific breed to get a list of rescue organizations. When you enter each specific breed link, you will see two hyperlinks; 1) "Learn About (specific breed)" and 2) a link to a list of national breed-specific rescue organizations.

I clicked on the letter 'L' for Labrador Retrievers, as they are one of the most popular breeds in North America. I thought they would have multiple rescue organizations dedicated to the breed. They did not. There was, however, a hyperlink to "Learn about Labrador Retrievers (and breeding standards)." Under rescue organizations is a link to the Labrador Retriever Club, Inc. This club is the only organization officially recognized by the American Kennel Club as the national parent club of the Labrador retriever. Unbelievably, the link directs you back to the AKC website.

Things get even more confusing on the AKC website when you read: "The AKC Rescue Network is the largest network of dog rescue groups in the country and was officially recognized by the American Kennel Club in late 2013." In reality, it's my understanding, they compiled a list of private rescue groups, encouraged rescue groups to register, and then gave themselves an award. It's ridiculous for the AKC to make such claims. If the AKC truly wants to help rescue dogs, rather than downloading the responsibility to private charitable rescue organizations run by volunteers, they should encourage every one of their registered breeders to take back their product, rehome it themselves, and provide evidence of rehoming to the AKC on a monthly basis.

THE CANADIAN KENNEL CLUB (CKC.CA)

As of October 2022, I could not find any assistance or even a reference on the Canadian Kennel Club (CKC) website offering any support for rescue organizations, but I read their blog titled *The Dish: Get The Inside Scoop*. A posting from April 9, 2021, 'Canada's Most Popular Breeds 2020', caught my eye.

"2020 was a year unlike any we've seen before. Amid lockdowns, shutdowns, travel bans, masks and social distancing many people experienced joy in the form of a new puppy. 56,805 purebred pups were welcomed into new homes and registered with the Canadian Kennel Club last year. If you compare that number of puppies to the previous year's 37,890 you will realize just how many more puppies we registered last year (+18,915). The allowance of working from home that many companies adopted allowed thousands of dog lovers to buy and train puppies last year. Their warm little hearts were no doubt a great source of comfort in a very unsettling year."

I would urge the CKC to contact each home those 56,805 purebred dogs went to and count how many have been surrendered to shelters and rescue organizations, as people went back to work, traveled, socialized, and enrolled their children in after-school and weekend activities. They should also do the same for calendar year 2021 and 2022. Maybe then they would offer some sort of assistance to rescue organizations that take in CKC registered dogs. Furthermore, the CKC should do an inventory check each and every year to ensure the registered breeders that produce the product, which the CKC receives a fee from, are not filling up shelters and rescue organizations. My gut tells me the number of dogs surrendered would be astonishing to the CKC.

FAMILY PET

My final question to Kennel Clubs is; why does a dog, bought as a family pet that will never be bred or entered in a dog show, have to meet such exacting and even punitive standards of the specific breed? I cannot make sense of the demands on the many varied breeds if they are well loved family pets that are going to chase a ball, slobber on a couch, go for a swim, maybe enjoy some agility classes, sleep in front of the fire and hang out with their family. Who cares if their tale isn't docked or their ears are not perfect? I don't think it will make a family, or myself, love the dog any less.

DESIGNER DOG KENNEL CLUBS

There is plenty of information to be found about hybrid, designer, boutique, new-breed, pure wannabes, mixed, or crossbreed clubs, but I found the information uncomfortable. Reading through the material and seeing statements such as "various stages of development, in between, or not yet established," made me very concerned for the dogs being bred. Suffice it to say, I feel designer dog breeders are a significant problem, especially when purebred or mixed-breed dogs are already sitting in shelters and rescue organizations across North America.

When designer breeders need to explain, as an example, that their Goldendoodle (Golden Retriever/Poodle mix) as an F1 (one parent was a purebred Poodle and the other parent was a purebred Golden Retriever) or F1B (bred from an F1 Goldendoodle and either 100% Poodle or a 100% Golden Retriever) maybe designer breeders simply need to drop the fancy numerical codes for their dogs and simply call it what it is, a mixed breed dog.

I know many people who own wonderful Goldendoodles. I may adopt one someday, understanding it is a mixed breed dog.

Hit television series such as *The Handmaid's Tale* (Season 3, episode 1) only complicate matters when they state Goldendoodles are hypoallergenic. Our society is in need of correcting misinformation and false news regarding dog allergens. It is my understanding that all dogs produce dander (i.e., allergens) so it is very difficult to state or promote any dog as hypoallergenic.

ANIMAL RESCUE ORGANIZATIONS NOT SUPPORTED

Some breeders, but not all, take their dogs back. It is disappointing that kennel clubs do not recognize the problems they are perpetuating. They could support and control the critical role played by rescue organizations by taking back their bred dogs. I feel it's time for all breeders (registered, not registered, dog farms and backyard breeders) to be accountable for the products they produce. It's long past time.

Another sad reality is operators of mass dog farms and BYBs do not support animal rescuers. The majority of irresponsible breeders do not take their dogs back as returns. If a family can no longer care for the dog, they will often contact the breeder, where they may quickly learn that these businesses treat their dogs as products and not as living souls. The result is that animal rescue organizations and shelters are forced to take in the surrendered dogs. When you adopt from a responsible rescue, most times your adoption contract will stipulate that if you can no longer care for the dog, the organization will guarantee they will take the dog back. These organizations take on a lifetime responsibility for the dogs they rescue.

Another sad fact is that mass dog farms and BYBs will often dump defective dogs, especially dogs too old to breed. They may abandon them in the woods, on country roads, take them to be euthanized, or simply shoot them. Yet, these unscrupulous breeders continue to produce unhealthy dogs. So around and around we go, with no end in sight, leaving rescue organizations to clean up the ugly mess left behind.

You do not need to be an animal lover to be aware of large-scale breeding operations or BYBs. The media constantly highlights these organizations when one of the farms or rings has been raided by authorities, resulting in the dogs being seized. The pictures are always the same: deplorable.

ONLY QUALITY PEOPLE BREED QUALITY DOGS

If you are buying a pup, please ensure you know the health and welfare of the breeding dogs left behind. Their lives depend on your research and scrutiny. You cannot rely solely on what you see on the internet or social media. Both puppies and breeding dogs' lives depend on your due diligence.

To protect breeding dogs and puppies, you must research the breeder in advance. Make sure you are dealing with a preservation breeder. You do not want to line the pockets of a terrible breeder. A preservation breeder produces high quality, healthy dogs. You must be able to meet the breeding dogs and tour the facility. Ask if they do genetic testing to ensure they produce healthy dogs; how often they breed the females; are the dogs kept indoors; and are they treated like cherished family members?

Ask the breeder at what age the pups leave the mother, and what happens to the mother dogs when they can no longer breed. The breeder should also offer health guarantees. Avoid breeders who only give refunds if the puppy is returned as they may euthanize it.

A great breeder will offer you references, and one of those references will be their veterinarian. But don't stop there. Call veterinary clinics in the area and ask if they have had any experience with the breeder. Call local shelters and rescues and ask if any breeder's dogs were surrendered or abandoned into their care. There are ethical breeders to be found, but you must do your homework first. A great breeder protects, knows and documents the bloodline and lineage of the dogs they produce. A great breeders loves the breed, nurtures the puppies, provides a clean, sanitary environment for breeding and pre-screens buyers. These breeders will also take back one of their dogs if you can no longer care for it.

A great breeder may even reach out to a rescue for help rehoming a retired breeding dog or a puppy. Again, these are wonderful breeders that care about their dogs.

RESCUE MISSION

*"We cannot solve our problems
with the same thinking we used when we created them."*
~Albert Einstein~

Rescue dogs are not an advocate's obsession; they are their mission. People involved in animal advocacy believe dogs need substantial protection. A domesticated social animal like a dog, which has done so much to enrich the lives of humans, deserves better care and attention.

All breeders—registered, unregistered, large-scale, or backyard—need to be held accountable for the product they produce, especially the unhealthy dogs they sell. Large-scale breeding facilities need to be shut down forever. Social media platforms need to be monitored, and it should be made illegal to import and transport large shipments of puppies across international borders. Regulations, oversight, and control must be increased and enforced because dogs pay the price with their lives.

Ethical breeders do not have to worry about enforcement. They produce healthy, social dogs. They also agree to take back a dog if the consumer can no longer care for it. These breeders do not want their dogs going to a shelter or rescue—they take responsibility for every dog they produce.

It should be noted that rescues may reach out to a good breeder from time to time. The rescue may have questions, such as feeding and exercise requirements, if they receive a dog of a breed they have never cared for in the past. A great breeder would offer as much information and insight as possible to support the dog even if it wasn't one of the dogs bred in their business. A great breeder cares about the breed.

"Unconditional love is as close
as your nearest shelter."
~unknown~

CALVIN

"If the kindest of souls were rewarded with the longest lives, dogs would outlive us all."
~Ricky Gervais~

After an intensive investigation, authorities seized Calvin and several other dogs from a breeder. They discovered Calvin was a special needs boy who would require an extraordinary home, and they found one for him. Sadly, Calvin was deaf, blind in his left eye, and had only partial vision in his right eye. Irresponsible breeders euthanize dogs like Calvin. Or they sell the dogs as bait dogs to illegal fighting rings. It is sad but true.

The rescue organization accepted many applications for Calvin, and one woman in particular was very interested in him. She and her daughter drove four hours to meet Calvin. They were stunned by the overflowing parking lot when they arrived, but they didn't give up hope. They entered the shelter and played with Calvin for several hours. Many people had applied for the

THE UGLY SIDE OF DOG BREEDING

pup, and they tried to convince the volunteers that their home would be the perfect fit for little Calvin.

The woman and her daughter left the shelter feeling confident the organization would find the perfect home for little Calvin. And two days later, her phone rang; the shelter had selected her home. She cried her eyes out, jumped in her car, and went to collect Calvin.

Although Calvin was a special needs boy, he was a typical puppy in every possible way. He was full of beans, excitable, loveable, active, and affectionate. Calvin ate socks, got in the garbage, ripped up toys, and raced around the house until it was time to collapse for a puppy nap. He was a happy, free-spirited, well-loved dog.

Calvin's family taught him their homemade brand of sign language commands for sit, down, come here, and good boy. Calvin was a quick learner; he was a brilliant boy.

Calvin struggled with the inside stairs as a young dog because of his vision impairment. The hardwood floors were the same color as the stairs, so they blended together. He'd make his way upstairs but wait patiently for his mom to bring him back down. As he matured, the stairs became easier for him to navigate.

At one point, Calvin's mom decided to hire a trainer. She wanted to ensure Calvin had the best skills possible to keep him safe and happy. The experienced trainer could not believe Calvin's intelligence and said Calvin paid more attention than dogs that can hear. The trainer told Calvin's mom she was doing a fantastic job, and the way she modified the training was working for the young dog.

Calvin's mom was heartbroken when he lost all sight in his only good eye a year after he was adopted. Calvin was blind and deaf, but that didn't slow him down. He had a fierce little spirit, and he was determined to move forward. Friends would say they didn't realize Calvin was blind and deaf because he still jumped on the couch to snuggle next to them and playfully show off his favorite toys. He was a happy, delightful little guy.

Calvin's family had to teach him a new way to communicate, so they taught him touch commands. For example, if they touched his chest, he should lie down. Two pats on his head told him he was a good boy. Calvin was a quick learner.

Although Calvin was now blind and deaf, he still ran five kilometers a few times a week with his mom. Calvin loved to run, and his mom didn't want to take that away from him, so Calvin ran on a leash with the complete trust he was safe.

As heartbroken as his mom was—his vision loss was extremely hard on her—she accepted that this was Calvin's new normal. He was with her 24/7, and it didn't matter what she was doing. She could be quilting, sewing, or eating peanut butter toast; Calvin was by her side. She knew that Calvin loved to swim, so she bought him a doggy lifejacket and an extra-long leash. When she put the life jacket on him, he would get very excited and lead her to the path to the beach. Calvin would stop at the entrance, not four feet before or three feet after, but at the exact spot at which they had entered many times. This act alone brought great comfort to Calvin's mom, knowing he still had an excellent quality of life.

Calvin didn't wallow in self-pity when he lost his sight. He could still find his toy box, and he still loved car rides. His mom had a vest made for him with "Blind & Deaf" printed on the side. Calvin wore the vest when he was on one of his sniff adventures with his mom, and she didn't care how long those journeys took; Calvin enjoyed them, and she rejoiced in his happiness.

Calvin lived a full and happy life with his devoted family for two and a half years until he became sick. They rushed Calvin to his veterinary clinic, and the staff lovingly monitored him for two days. Sadly, Calvin passed away, leaving his mother devastated and overwhelmed. She felt angry with the situation as Calvin was taken too early from her and her family. She felt it was unfair to Calvin given how much he thrived in her home, even with his disabilities. She went to the darkest place she had ever been in her life after losing Calvin.

As time moved on, she decided to help a local rescue group by fostering dogs. She wanted to be part of the dog's journey. She continues her mission today, even though she has two adoptive rescue dogs, one of whom is deaf.

Calvin's story and life are much too familiar within many rescue communities, especially when it comes to selfish dog breeders. Breeders that don't care about the welfare of the breeding dog and knowingly sell disabled dogs like Calvin.

THE UGLY SIDE OF DOG BREEDING

Luckily, Calvin secured a wonderful home where he thrived, and they never let his disabilities get in the way of him living his life to the fullest. All dogs should be so fortunate.

TOBY

"Enjoy the little things in life because one day you'll look back and realize they were the big things."
~Robert Brault~

A mass dog breeding operator heartlessly tossed Toby away. He was the runt (smallest) of a litter, so they didn't want to use him as a breeding dog because they probably couldn't make much money off him. He was listed on Kijiji, and he bounced around among five different homes in seven months. Toby's adoptive dad kept track of him on social media as he very much wanted to save him. He instinctively knew Toby was in danger.

When he could finally track Toby down, his instincts were right; the dog was in a nasty situation. He jumped in his car and drove for hours to rescue the little dog. When he finally found Toby, the dog was dangerously underweight with little fur. What little fur he had was wispy thin, and it could not protect him from the sub-zero winter temperatures. The man who had Toby (the fifth owner), had callously tied him outside in freezing temperatures to a cold metal fence. He told Toby's dad: "He's not housetrained, he doesn't listen, and he's not cuddly. He's tied outside because I just had my floors refinished."

Toby's new forever dad took one look at the scared little dog, picked him up, and brought him home. He discovered immediately upon returning home that Toby loved other dogs, because his new dad already had a couple of dogs at home. But poor Toby had never been allowed to bond with humans. His dad knew how vital those first few months of socialization are for dogs, but he wouldn't give up on Toby.

Little Toby initially struggled, psychologically, in his new home. He would hide behind the couch when his loving dad walked into the room. Toby would also watch, from the top of the stairs, while his dad softly stroked his other dogs when watching TV or listening to music. Little Toby would fall asleep at the top of the stairs, but he couldn't trust his dad, not quite yet.

After three months of living together, his dad decided he had to do something to help little Toby learn to trust him. He had given Toby all the space he needed to settle into his home. He watched Toby play at length with his doggy siblings, but he desperately wanted to build a trusting relationship with Toby.

His dad lay on the floor in the living room, on his back, with treats in his open hands. He lay there for hours with Toby watching intently but struggling with what to do. Finally, Toby inched a little closer, and in the span of a few hours, he got close enough for his dad to scratch him under his little chin. It was probably the first time in Toby's life that a human had touched him with affection, and Toby loved it. He laid his little head down beside the first person in the world that had ever been kind to him, and he hasn't moved his head for seven years. His dad is his favorite person, and he lavishes his rescuer with love and attention every day and night.

Now that Toby was so happy, he was given a job; he went to the radio station most days with his dad, sitting on his dad's lap all day. Toby has also finally decided he loves country music, and his tail wags wildly when he hears Miranda Lambert singing.

Toby is a happy boy, but he won't eat, chase a squirrel, go through a door, or jump on the bed until his dad gives his approval. His dad did not teach or train him to look for approval. Toby simply wants to please his dad because he loves him to death. Toby also knows how good he has it in his wonderful home. At the top of the list are his dad, his two fur siblings, and his radio station dog job. He is now living the kind of life every dog should have, and he will never forget his previous lonely life.

Toby's dad believes that Toby has the kindest soul and says he wears his little heart on his sleeve. Toby hopes Miranda Lambert can one day see that heart, and he promises to let her kiss him.

WINNIE

*"Scratch a dog, and you'll find
a permanent job."*
~Franklin P. Jones~

Winnie started her life as a breeding dog at a large-scale breeding operation. She was initially the runt of a litter at the mill. To this day, she only weighs thirteen pounds, making her very petite. She found her forever home and is now fourteen years young. This sweet-faced girl is not food-motivated; her faithful dad says she is kindness-motivated. Not surprisingly, she has her dad wrapped around her little paw.

She sleeps with her dad every night, and she must be carried up and down the stairs. Not because she can't do it on her own, but because she's a little princess. If lightning or thunder cracks, she'll swiftly clear the stairs on her own. But of course, all of that is forgotten; minutes after the storm clears, she returns to being carried.

RECYCLED LOVE

This girl does not and will not chase squirrels. She loves other dogs, especially large dogs. She does not have the small dog mentality; she sees herself as a large dog. She will not play with toys; the only exception is a little yellow bunny that has lost its stuffing and is now in two pieces. The bunny is also fourteen years old, and it came with her when her dad initially brought her home.

For such a sweet, angelic, delicate little dog, this girl can snore. Her dad is convinced Winnie snores louder than he does. Too bad they don't make nose-strips for dogs because her dad has a demanding career on radio. He's up at the crack of dawn each weekday morning to head to the station, so he needs his sleep. But he never complains because Winnie is the center of his world.

Winnie loves to go on walks with her dad. He enjoys watching her discover the world around her and rub that sweet face on every dandelion or blade of grass. She's a bathing beauty who loves to lie in the hot sun. But her dad will gently pick her up when she starts panting and place her in the shade. Her dad has a Jeep, and she loves to go for drives, but she must ride shotgun. Her dad is also a Ducati rider, but it doesn't have a sidecar, so she stays home when he drives the bike. She doesn't mind, even though she doesn't need any beauty rest; she sleeps and snores until he returns home.

She has one roughhousing habit for such a delicate little dog. She likes to lie on the carpet with her front paws outstretched, and dad must drag her around. She's obsessed with this tradition, and her dad doesn't mind. As long as Winnie is happy, her dad is happy because Winnie makes his world very cheerful.

Another fun fact about Winnie; she reserves her belly rubs exclusively for her dad. Other than that, her belly is no-touch territory. She doesn't get mad; she simply will not tolerate it. Her dad saved her many years ago, so he must come first on all levels in her little world.

Her little world was rocked by a health scare a few years ago. She developed seizures that would cause her to fall, and her pulse became dangerously shallow. Her dad raced her to the hospital, where they did brain scans, whole-body scans, ran multiple other tests, and they put her on an intravenous drip. All tests returned negative, and the hospital called her the little miracle. She's completely healthy now, much to her dad's relief, outside of a bit of a cough.

Winnie and her dad live an extraordinary life together. They look out for each other and have snoring contests at night.

PIPSQUEAK

"The bond with a true dog is as lasting as the ties of this earth will ever be."
~Konrad Lorenz~

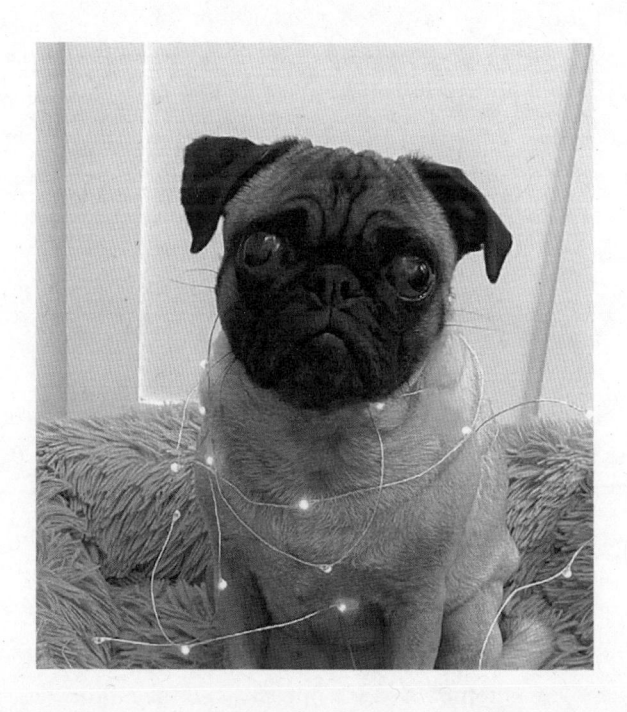

This little beauty is a purebred Pug named Pipsqueak, but her parents call her Pip or Gremlin because she's full of beans. A lovely young couple adopted her and she became the center of their world, especially her dad's world.

Pip had a hard start in life with a backyard breeder. When she was a puppy, something went wrong, and her front right leg was broken. The breeder did not have her leg medically corrected, and it was a nasty break. The leg was shattered along the growth plate. When the couple adopted her at six months old, they took her to a top veterinary hospital to evaluate the tiny leg.

Instead of removing the leg, they performed extensive surgery and strongly recommended physiotherapy for Pip. This little girl took to the therapy with great energy, including hydrotherapy (an underwater treadmill).

Pip now gets around perfectly and is very capable at tormenting her fur brother and sister. She rules the house with her positive energy. Her mom said Pip could go from zero to one hundred in a split second, so food that hits the floor never stands a chance. This also means that brother and sister never get a chance at the five-second rule for floor-food.

For such a little girl, food makes her world go around. Her parents even planted a raspberry bush for her, but she still helps herself to everything else in the garden. She has a green thumb and will help her mom dig holes for new plants each spring. Her mom lovingly refers to her as her "little badness."

Pip loves to help her parents in the kitchen. It's not unusual for her parents to find her standing on the open dishwasher door. Pip loves to help with the pre-clean cycle by licking all the plates and bowls. Pip will do anything to help her parents out, especially if food is involved. She's the best girl ever, with a marvellously massive spirit.

Pip has one favorite toy. It's a rubber ball that looks like a Covid protein. She has played and chewed it so much, it has begun to disintegrate. Her mom bought her a new one, but Pip wanted nothing to do with it, so her mom got creative. She sewed one-half of the new ball to one-half of the remaining old ball, and Pip has begun to play with it again. Her mom calls the toy her "Frankenstein Ball." Pip is very fortunate to have such devoted parents because her life changed forever when she was two years old.

Her parents came home for lunch one day, and they immediately noticed that Pip was not acting like herself. They rushed her to the veterinarian, where they learned Pip had gone blind. They instantly made an appointment with an ophthalmologist four hours away. They discovered at the clinic that both of Pip's retinas were deteriorating, and they had become detached. They were heartbroken, but Pip, being such a bundle of energy, didn't let her blindness slow her down. She still torments her fur siblings, going so far as grabbing both food and toys from her brother's mouth. She's the true essence of the annoying little sister. She's a remarkable girl with a trouble-loving, spunky, extraordinarily outgoing personality.

THE UGLY SIDE OF DOG BREEDING

When Pip is quiet, her mom says she is the snuggliest pup. She's super chill and loves nothing more than to be cuddled on the couch. Every beauty queen needs their beauty rest.

Little Pip is the by-product of bad breeding, but luckily she landed in a forever home with a family who loves her and takes great care of her—for the rest of her life. Pip, as they say, is living her best life possible. She's like a bit of chew-barka to her siblings, and she's the apple of her parent's eyes. What dog could want more? Well, Pip does. She wants more food and more time to annoy her fur siblings. And don't touch her Frankenstein Ball.

LITTLE

"Even the largest avalanche is triggered by small things."
~Vernor Vinge~

This toy poodle's story began long before she was rescued. She was part of a breeding establishment's business for at least eight years. During those eight years, it is not known if she was ever let out of her crate or if she ever felt grass under her feet. The day she was rescued was probably the first time she had someone kind touch her.

Her breeder was under investigation after multiple complaints had been lodged with the authorities. He fell ill during the inquiry and ultimately surrendered all the breeding dogs. A woman, the lead investigator for animal cruelty complaints, was involved in the examination, surrender, and intake process for all the dogs. Someone on her team reached into a crate and handed her a matted mess of a little emaciated dog. They did not know if the dog was male or female. They didn't even know which end was her head because the dog was cemented with urine and feces.

While shaving the little dog, they discovered she was female. But they had to stop shaving her as her skin was in terrible condition from a lifetime of neglect, and she was pretty fragile. They bathed her, and she went home with her rescuer, who named her Little because she was the smallest of all the dogs surrendered. Her adoptive mom does not know how many litters Little produced, but she had multiple puppies over many years.

Little is now fifteen years old, and she's living the best life ever, even though the first eight years of her life were appalling. Little sleeps all day, on the big bed, when her mom is out saving other animals. In the evening, she spends her time in her mother's loving arms. She refuses to eat until her mom comes home, demonstrating how emotionally devoted she is to the woman who saved and enriched her life.

Little's owner has an emotionally crushing, physically demanding, yet gratifying, career. She has performed many animal cruelty investigations, and has been on countless seizures, surrenders, and intakes. Police officers often have to protect her and her team during the most dangerous circumstances. Regardless, nothing will stop her from protecting helpless animals that need defending.

She also oversees and writes legal reports on animal investigations and is often in court, under oath, testifying about her experiences and what she has witnessed. I've seen her in action—she's intelligent, open, and sincere on the stand. Animals are lucky to have such a sensible and honest person on their side.

As Little has matured, she has lost most of her teeth, and she is still a bit anxious most days. Sometimes when dogs experience trauma early in life, it stays with them throughout their whole lives. Luckily, she has a mom dedicated to ensuring her safety and who also understands the trauma she lived with for an agonizing eight years.

Little may not know or understand what her mom does daily, but she loves her. People often say the best gifts come in small packages. I think Little's mom would happily agree with that statement.

CHEWIE

"Every act of kindness is a piece of love we leave behind."
~Paul Williams~

Chewie is a handsome, fun-loving, energetic seven-year-old yellow Labrador Retriever with a story to tell. His story involves many kind people who came together to provide him with the life every dog should be living.

His narrative began as a puppy at a breeder's home. The mother dog, who lived outside, had given birth. Four weeks later, during a blistering winter storm, the breeder collected the mother dog and her puppies. He brought them inside but discovered the next day that he had left one puppy behind. Overnight, the puppy's paws had become frozen to the ground, resulting in the loss of his pads on all four feet to frostbite. The puppy was Chewie.

As the breeder could not sell a damaged puppy, he gave Chewie to a family. For four long years, they let Chewie hop around like a kangaroo.

THE UGLY SIDE OF DOG BREEDING

When the family decided to move overseas, they talked about euthanizing him. A wonderful woman who operates a rescue organization reached out to Chewie's family and asked if they would consider surrendering him into her care. They agreed, and this is where Chewie's life began.

The rescue organization's veterinarian immediately put Chewie on pain medication, and then they devised a medical plan to help him walk. The plan included hydrotherapy to teach Chewie how to use all four legs in a natural motion. Then, a custom-made two-wheel cart was created, and Chewie took to it like a dog to a bone.

Chewie's rehabilitation took a long time, but when he was ready to find a forever home, the organization was patient and found the best possible family. Now Chewie has a mom and dad that adore him and a doggy sibling he idolizes.

Chewie's parents fell in love with his positive attitude and his tail, which never stops wagging. Of course, they credit the rescue organization for all the care and love they provided Chewie throughout his rehabilitation.

Chewie loved to race through their home with his wheels on, chasing his puppy sibling. But sometimes the puppy would turn sharply, and he'd tip over on his wheels. His parents started to wonder if there was anything else they could do to help get Chewie even more mobile. They spoke to their vet, who decided to investigate what else they could do. An idea emerged, and the veterinarian set a detailed plan in motion. Chewie had reconstructive surgery on his paws, and voila —Chewie can now walk without his wheels.

He goes on many outdoor adventures with his family, but his favorite is camping. His family is so devoted to caring for him, they never take a vacation because they never want Chewie to feel abandoned. When they go for bike rides, Chewie has a little buggy that hooks onto the bike just in case he gets tired. He's a sensitive boy who doesn't like it when his puppy sister chases the cat. His parents said he isn't the typical Labrador Retriever when it comes to food; he's more people-motivated. I encourage you to follow him on Facebook—his page is called "Charming Chewie."

Chewie, against all odds, is living an extraordinary life. His parents pull out all the stops to keep him happy and healthy forever. It sounds like a fairy tale with a happily-ever-after ending for sweet Chewie.

A LOVING FOREVER HOME

"Second hand animals make first-class pets."
~unknown~

Adopting a dog can be compared to online dating, as both relationships usually begin with a single photo. But you would never commit the next ten to fifteen years of your life to someone based solely on an image you saw online. The same should be the case when you consider adopting a dog. A single photo with a few sentences describing a dog's personality cannot possibly tell the complete story.

SPEAK WITH VOLUNTEERS

The first step in the adoption process is a conversation with the rescue organization or shelter staff. They can answer all your questions because they have lived with the dog, loved it, and cared for it while waiting to find the perfect forever home. These volunteers know everything about the dog, and they can provide valuable information to you and your family. In most cases, these volunteers will have significant input into who would qualify to adopt and provide a forever home for the dog.

Success rates for animal rescue adoptions are very high, unlike online dating. A responsible rescue organization will publish a truthful, candid, and accurate dog biography, and photos and/or videos. The dog profile will include crucial information such as whether the dog likes cats or children, has low or high energy, and if they can live with other dogs. The profile will consist of tips such as "the dog needs a fenced-in yard," "they suffer from separation anxiety," and how they act around strangers. The information contained in the dog's biography is meant to highlight the dog's personality, character, and temperament to help potential adopters find a compatible rescue dog.

PUREBRED RESCUE DOGS

Individuals looking to adopt a specific breed often reach out to rescues and shelters. A misconception concerning rescue dogs is that the dogs are most likely mixed-breed dogs, but that is not the case. Many dogs waiting for forever homes are purebred dogs of every shape, color, and size. There are also many purebred rescue groups devoted to rescuing specific breeds.

THE MEET-UP

Rescue organizations and shelters encourage potential adopters to meet the dog after filling out an application. But, firstly and most importantly, the dog will be given ample time to settle into foster care or shelter life. Some dogs will need a significant amount of time to allow rescuers to understand the dog's individual needs, while others require less time to understand their personalities. The dogs past experiences will also dictate how long they need to decompress or adjust and allow their personalities to emerge.

THE APPLICATION

Anyone can buy a dog, but not everyone can adopt one. Rescues and shelters pre-screen adopters and conduct many open and candid conversations through their application process. As a potential adopter, it is essential to be truthful throughout the process. Rescue organizations want to prepare both the adopter and the dog for a successful lifelong relationship.

That potential relationship begins with the adoption application. People often find the two- or three-page application time-consuming or cumbersome because of the detailed questions. Many ask, "If you have dogs looking for homes, why don't you just give me one?" The hard truth is that some dogs are not a good match for every home, and some homes are not a good match for every dog. Just because you read a few lines about a dog, saw its sweet picture, and believe the dog would suit you, you may find it is not a good match. Think about dating shows like *The Bachelor* and *Millionaire Matchmaker*, and their histories of epic failures. Rescue organizations successfully place their dogs in loving forever homes because they put considerable energy into the process, including an extensive adoption application. At the heart of the process is a dog that has already been removed from the only home it has ever known, and that home may have been a good one or sadly, a bad one.

The first step in finding a perfect home for a dog begins with the application. The application will usually emphasize the group's policies and expectations for adoption. Many progressive rescue organizations include personal rules. The rules may include only hiring trainers who use positive reinforcement training, not using a trainer who instructs with prong or shock collars, and not using electric fences to contain the dogs. These rescue organizations will not place an animal with an adopter supporting abusive training or containment practices.

THE HOME VISIT

Another critical step in the adoption process may include a home visit. You may feel this requirement is unnecessary or intrusive, but the organization must be confident that the dog will be living in a safe environment.

When I conducted home visits, I usually brought a jar of my homemade jam to help soothe potential adopters' stress. During home visits, which lasted about fifteen minutes, I was not looking to judge if the person was a good housekeeper or trendy decorator. I walked through the home to ensure the dog would be going to a stable and safe environment. Again, it's all about setting the dog up for successful adoption.

Rescue organizations will do everything possible not to let the dog down a second time. The last thing any rescue or shelter wants to see is a dog returned—this is known as a boomerang dog. Society has already let these dogs down and they need to be protected from further stress or disappointment.

"HAPPY GOTCHA DAY"

The best step in the adoption process is being approved as an adopter and bringing your new four-legged best friend into your home. Settling a newly adopted dog into your home is the last and final step in adopting. This final step sets both you and the dog up for success. You will already have plenty of helpful information about the dog's personality traits. Still, there are a few additional steps you can take to help the dog during its transition, which will be different for every dog. Your home will have unfamiliar smells and new routines to figure out, so be patient and sympathetic as the dog may have some anxiety during this phase. Whether the dog came from a foster home or a shelter, the transition period will be different for each dog.

For dogs rescued from a hoarding situation or a life tied outside, hardwood, carpet, or tiled flooring might be new to them. They may even find stairs confusing. Sounds from microwaves, blow dryers, vacuum cleaners, and doorbells can create anxiety for a new dog. Introduce the dog to anything new in slow stages and take baby steps. You certainly do not want to overwhelm the dog. Dogs surrendered from a home environment generally settle more quickly than dogs from poor previous lives. They truly only need patience and understanding.

THE HONEYMOON PERIOD

It may take at least six months for the dog to feel confident in a new home and new routines; however, some dogs settle much faster. To ensure a smooth transition for the new dog, keep your household routine as regular as possible for the first few weeks. Dogs thrive on routine and boundaries.

Have a dedicated spot that solely belongs to the dog, such as a comfortable couch or a well-placed dog bed. If your rescue dog came with a crate they love, put it somewhere in a room that is easy to access. Leave the crate door open so they can explore your home easily through the day. Toys and high-value treats should be plentiful initially because you want to strive to make all their first experiences with you very positive. I find having plenty of peanut butter on hand is helpful. Let's face it; peanut butter makes everything better.

A LOVING FOREVER HOME

Set up a strict schedule for feeding, walks, and bedtime. You may find your new dog is exhausted in the beginning. Stress is mentally draining for dogs who rely on instinct to guide them through life. Be patient and understanding and give them an overdose of praise.

Remember, you are not alone; you always have access to volunteers at the rescue or shelter where you adopted your dog. These individuals are on your side, and they're just a phone call away with helpful advice to support you and the dog moving forward.

First and foremost, have fun. Take pictures and videos that you can share with friends and family to show how well your dog is doing in their new environment. And don't forget to commemorate your "Happy Gotcha Day" every year. As most rescue dogs' birthdays are unknown, your Gotcha Day, the day you brought your rescue dog home, should be celebrated. You have a lifetime of memories to look forward to and many adventures to explore with your new best friend. Take a deep breath, enjoy the experience, and revel in the positive emotions—you saved a life.

"People who say money can't buy happiness,
have never paid an adoption fee."
~unknown~

TUK

*"Once you have had a wonderful dog,
a life without one is a life diminished."*
~Dean Koontz~

Tuk is a hunky and handsome purebred chocolate Labrador retriever. You may recognize his sweet face, as he is on the cover of this book. Many people love him dearly, especially his adoptive mom. His previous owners unceremoniously dumped him in rescue and heartlessly said, "Either take the dog, or we'll euthanize him today." They said he was nine years old, they were moving, and did not want to take him along.

Luckily, the organization had an available foster home, so they took possession of Tuk, and a volunteer (who also became his foster mom) picked him up. She sensed immediately that Tuk had a charming personality and gentle demeanor. She knew she would never allow him to leave her home, so she adopted him. She already owned a wonderful rescue dog, but she made room in her home and heart for Tuk. His lovely, calm, sweet, comical personality blossomed under her loving care.

Not surprisingly—this happens all too often—Tuk was surrendered without food, bowls, toys, beds, or anything that would have helped him during his transition. His foster mom made sure Tuk was more than comfortable in her home, and her other dog generously shared his toys with him.

The foster mom could tell that Tuk had probably never been to a veterinarian. He was not neutered, his nails were too long, and he desperately needed a bath and grooming. At his first veterinary appointment, it was discovered that the surrendering family had lied about his age. He was most likely a young three or four years old, not nine as they had said. The rescue organization lovingly and unselfishly looked after all of Tuk's veterinary care. He was neutered after he settled into his foster home. He was also vaccinated and given flea treatments and everything else he needed to keep him healthy and happy.

Tuk's an easy-going dreamy boy, and if he had been born a human, he would most definitely have been another George Clooney. Women swoon for Tuk, and I know this because I am one of those women.

Tuk's adoptive mom has a demanding career as the head of technology for five regional schools. She often took him to work, and he became a favorite visitor at one of the schools.

Tuk eventually became a school therapy dog, and he worked with special needs kids two days a week. Some of the children had autism or behavioral issues, and they became highly attached to his visits as he has such a gentle disposition. The school acknowledged Tuk's positive impression on the children, and they welcomed him into the school as often as he could make it.

The school bought him a little jacket and embroidered his name alongside Therapy Dog. When Tuk put the coat on in the morning, he got very excited because he knew he was going to school. He would lie quietly beside the children at school and let them read aloud to him. He never passed judgment if a child mispronounced a word or stuttered. He was just happy to be with the kids.

Often Tuk would lie under a child's desk during the day, never leaving their side. Kids were encouraged to do their homework with him, and the kids would get rewarded points for good behavior. These points allowed them to take Tuk for a walk, or play fetch or tug of war with him. Tuk usually won the tug of war games, and the kids didn't mind.

Tuk's mom was always exceptionally busy at work, and she would often find him at the end of the day at the principal's office. She always laughed and asked him what he had done wrong, but he never did anything wrong. Teachers often brought him to the principal's office for a break, and they even bought him a couple of doggy gates so he couldn't wander down the hall back to the classroom. Tuk plays such an essential and integral role for the children, so they decided to add a picture of him in the school yearbook, wearing his unique custom-made school vest.

Considering Tuk's calm personality, his mom decided to enrol him in the official St. John Ambulance Course to become a registered Therapy Dog. Of course, he impressed the instructors and passed with flying colors.

Tuk is perfect in every way. He loves other dogs, cats, kids, and people, and if he met a giraffe, he'd love him, too. He loves car rides, swimming, hiking, sunbeams, and lying in puddles, but his favorite is dirt baths. Tuk will find and roll in dirt for as long as possible. He is also obsessed with food, all food.

He is now nine or ten years old, and for the last five years, he has been a beloved member of his family and community. His mom has bent over backwards to ensure he is happy, healthy, and comfortable. When he was diagnosed with painful hip dysplasia, she lovingly paid for the surgery and nursed him back to health.

To think his previous owners had threatened to euthanize him is unbelievable. Although Tuk has ageing hips, he still chases tennis balls, takes dirt baths, and helps children. He is the poster boy of success stories for rescue.

RAIDER

*"Dogs have a way of finding the people who need them,
Filling an emptiness we don't even know we have."*
~Thom Jones~

Sometimes a dog in desperate need of a safe home finds one, all by themselves. This is precisely what Raider the charming and adorable yellow Labrador Retriever did; he picked his own forever home.

At eight weeks old, a couple bought Raider from a breeder. They brought him home and instantly put him outside in a wire kennel run. This little guy lived outside without any protection from the elements; he did not have a bowl of water or even a regular feeding schedule. A neighbor entrenched in animal rescue kept a close eye on Raider. One miserable rainy day, she called the couple at their place of work. She spoke to them about Raider's lack of care; the result was that she took Raider to her home for the night.

A LOVING FOREVER HOME

The couple picked up Raider in the morning and promptly placed him back in the outside run. When winter arrived, they penned Raider in their damp basement. Raider's concerned neighbor kept the lines of communication open with his owners. As luck would have it, she worked with Raider's dad.

That spring, a For Sale sign went up on Raider's family's property. The worried neighbor took the initiative to ask if she could care for Raider while they moved, and they agreed. She broke the speed limit to go and pick up Raider and bring him to her home again.

Poor Raider was like a deer on ice inside her home because he had never experienced hardwood floors, stairs, tiles, or indoor living. She bathed him twice because he was stinky from being outside all the time and not cared for. She also house-trained dear Raider because he had never lived in anything but a cage. Ten days later, the owners called and said they were on their way to pick up "the dog."

Raider was so happy and settled for those ten days, as he had never experienced what it was like to be loved and be a valued member of a family. When the owners arrived, Raider refused to leave. They had to physically drag Raider out of the home; he had become comfortable in. Poor Raider squealed loudly in protest; it wasn't a barking sound he made, he screamed. To this day, the kind neighbor is still haunted by those unearthly sounds.

Amazingly, a week later, the owners called yet again to ask if she could look after Raider for the weekend, and of course she said yes. By Sunday night, they called and asked, "Do you want to keep him?" You can guess what her reply was.

Raider was barely one year old when he selected his perfect forever home, and it was the best home any dog could ever dream of. This little guy had no training; he did not know the commands for Sit or Down. He barely knew his name, but all that quickly changed under his loving adoptive mom's tender care. She threw every bit of her soul into that little man, and he thrived under her watchful eye. When he became gravely ill one month later, she nursed him back to health, and he never forgot. The two became inseparable.

Raider grew into a distinguished boy with a heart of gold and a delightful disposition. He loved swimming, hiking, and chasing a ball or whatever you had to offer. He just went with the flow. He lived eleven and a half years as a blessed, valued companion with the best dog-mom possible. She still says that Raider was the first dog to ever talk to her, and years later, he is still very much missed.

REDGY

"Life is a series of thousands of tiny miracles. Notice them."
~Roald Dahl~

This handsome little guy, a purebred Bichon Frise, was part of a massive large-scale breeding facility bust. The influx of dogs into the rescue organization was significant, leaving them no choice but to keep several of the rescued dogs in the basement. While at the shelter, every dog was lovingly examined by a veterinarian, given a bath by staff, fed, and placed in a fresh, clean crate.

    A young family of four desperately wanted to adopt a small dog. When they heard about the animals that had been seized, they contacted the shelter and met the dogs. The two little girls could not contain their excitement when they saw the little dog in his crate. He was pacing back and forth with a quirky little smile on his face. They were told he was somewhere between three and five years old. They fell in love with his silly overbite and one lazy eye. The little dog fell in love, too, because he started running circles in the crate when the girls got close. The family decided to adopt the dog and named him Redgy.

They brought him home and let him settle into life with their family. He knew he had been adopted by a lovely family as soon as he got home. The girls brushed his fur, took him on walks, and took turns feeding him. He was a comical and charming little guy with a long, curly, creamy-colored furry coat.

Two weeks after bringing him home, they took him to a groomer. Redgy's mom was shocked when she picked him up from the beauty parlour. She called her family and exclaimed, "Our dog is white!" Little Redgy had lived in such horrible conditions that his coat had become stained with years of dirt and filth. One trip to the groomer revealed a bright and shiny pure white coat.

Redgy was settling into family life perfectly. He was so happy to finally have a forever home of his own. The family wanted to take him to the veterinarian to look at his lazy eye, but his gaze was perfect, to everyone's surprise. The veterinarian said his vision problem could have resulted from malnutrition and living in a cramped crate. With proper nourishment, the vision had corrected itself. Redgy's family was delighted to hear the good news.

Although Redgy went to obedience classes, he did not need the training. He never jumped on the furniture, chewed anything inappropriate, chased squirrels, or reacted to other dogs; and he never played with or destroyed toys. His sister said, "Redgy was like the perfect, polite house guest."

Redgy's other sister said, "He was my mom's number one companion. She would put him in her bag when she went shopping. It was hilarious and adorable."

Redgy had many things that he loved dearly; one was car rides. If there was a passenger in the car, he'd lay quietly on that lap. If only the driver was in the car, he lay on the floor and fell asleep. He never hung his head out the window or barked at passing dogs. He was just happy to tag along for a drive.

As for food, he did not beg from the table or bother anyone when they were snacking on the couch. But if he heard the potato peeler come out of the utensil drawer, he'd hightail it to the kitchen. He was obsessed with potato, apple, and carrot peels.

A LOVING FOREVER HOME

Redgy lived his life following his family around the house for ten years. He'd sit patiently by the door when they were out. When they returned, he'd wait to see where they sat so that he could crawl up on someone's lap. When the girls were little, he would sleep beside their beds. As the girls grew up and moved out of the house, he advanced to sleeping between his mom and dad.

Redgy is what some people would refer to as a whatever dog. Nothing upset him. He went with the flow, loved his life, and was happy to hang with his family. If they had company over, that was fine with him. It meant more laps to sit on and people to fuss over him. If an elephant showed up at the front door, he would have taken it all in stride.

Redgy was this young family's first dog, and when they adopted him, they thought he was vision impaired. He certainly set the standard very high for any dog that followed him. He was the sweetest, most perfect dog, and he wasn't a rabble-rouser, but you better hide that pesky potato peeler.

ANGEL

"It is beautiful to express love and even more beautiful to feel it."
~Dejan Stojanovic~

This photogenic beauty, named Angel, travelled thousands of kilometers to find her perfect forever home. She was six years young and when adopted by a lovely couple. Her adoring mom said, "She's a super well-behaved girl who catches on quickly when learning new tricks. She's the perfect addition to our family."

Angel's family vet could tell she had been bred at least twice. Little is known about her past, but her family has promised her a very happy future.

This girl goes to doggy daycare full of positive energy, spreading her love among the other dogs. She can be found most days digging a large hole—she lies down and claims it for herself. If she isn't digging holes, she's playing tag or sliding down the colorful dog slide. She's very popular at doggy daycare, and she loves the attention.

She also loves puppies and children. Even with all that energy, she's an incredibly gentle and nurturing with souls much smaller than her. She has shown a slight interest in squirrels and cats, but her mom said she hadn't chased any. She's so gracious, she became a Therapy Dog—she passed the tests with flying colors, she also earned the Canine Good Neighbour Certification. She's an extraordinary girl, and as soon as anybody meets her, they fall in love with her.

Angel will do anything, and I mean anything, for a treat. She knows how to sit up pretty, bow, circle, and walk between your legs. Her mother has recently taught her yoga, and her favorite move is balancing on a pink yoga ball with all four feet. She's very athletic, and she excels at dock diving. Her mom has posted many pictures of Angel flying through the air, diving into the water. I don't think there's much in this world that Angel wouldn't attempt or succeed in accomplishing.

Angel has big, soft, comfy beds all over the house, but she usually picks the one closest to her mom. However, her mom must apologize from time to time when she's on the phone because Angel snores. Not soft little grunts: it's more like a blow-the-roof-off-your-house kind of snore. But she's so beautiful inside and out; she can be forgiven for the horrendously loud snoring. Angel, of course, makes snoring look good.

She's a very good girl when she's waiting for her food. She goes to her crate, which doesn't have a door, and waits for room service. She's a patient girl, deeply bonded to both her mom and dad. So much so, she won't get up in the morning until her dad gets out of bed.

Her parent's take her on ninety-minute hikes every day, and they also train one-on-one with her for at least fifteen minutes each day. Angel is brilliant and creative, so the training and long hikes help to keep this girl happy and content.

When you're as pretty as Angel, you don't need much grooming. She wakes up looking beautiful every day without any solid effort. When she needs a pedicure, she quietly lies down on the floor, and she is so relaxed, she almost falls asleep.

She also has an odd routine before she goes to sleep each night. It must be followed, or she doesn't settle down: her teeth must be brushed. She will stare at her parents before bedtime if they haven't brushed her pearly whites.

When her mom gets her toothbrush out, Angel will come up behind her, put her little head between her mom's knees and look up at her. This is the stance or position she takes every night to brush her teeth. Could this dog be any cuter? I don't think so.

She is flawless in her beauty, personality, and brain. If you're lucky, she'll show up in your yoga class sometime. She has excellent balance and does a very generous downward dog.

BROOKLYN

"Some people talk to animals. Not many listen though. That's the problem."
~A. A. Milne~

Brooklyn is a lovely, calm girl who was surrendered to rescue after living on a farm. She's a sheepdog mix with a sweet disposition who wants nothing other than your full attention. If she is not the center of every conversation, gathering, or family outing, she will let you know in the gentlest way. She adores her adoptive parents and thrives under their attention. Her mom and dad both have busy careers, and her mom is a top executive with a rescue organization. Suffice it to say; her mom proudly wears her rescue heart on her sleeve.

When Brooklyn was adopted, her parents noticed immediately that she didn't know how to play with toys. She'd gather them up as if she was guarding or watching over them. It must have been a leftover from living on a farm.

They had to teach her how to enjoy the world around her, and Brooklyn quickly discovered those perks, such as the best spot on the couch. She also developed a silly stunt to get off the couch; she rolls off it in slow motion every time. Her mother said she's an actual couch potato, and Brooklyn plays that role to the fullest every day.

Brooklyn is a quintessential Velcro dog who will paw at your arm if you stop petting her. She's also a pleaser and will do anything for your approval and praise. She has two doggy siblings who are often found in the backyard playing. She loves when her mom throws the ball for her siblings. They will run to fetch the ball, leaving Brooklyn behind, hogging all her mom's attention. Why in the world would Brooklyn ever run away from her mom? She wouldn't be able to pet her if she's too far away. She's a very clever girl.

She's such a lovable dog, only her mom can groom her. She tried taking her to a groomer, but Brooklyn chose to lay on her back for belly rubs instead. So her mom gave up and started grooming her at home, to Brooklyn's delight.

Brooklyn's parents have an in-ground pool, and Brooklyn loves to swim. But she will not walk or dive into the pool; she must be carried, and at ninety-eight pounds, it's a challenge for her parents. To her surprise, she once fell in the pool chasing a squirrel. Of course, she blamed the squirrel, and now she patrols the pool perimeter as a "No Squirrels Allowed" zone.

Brooklyn's mom tries to walk the dogs at different times and separately. On one walk with Brooklyn's sister, her mom noticed a dog running down the street. Her instinct was to get her dog home as fast as possible to help the roaming dog, and then she realized it was Brooklyn. She had jumped the fence to go and find her beloved mom. This girl also figured out how to open the garden gate, so her parents had to add a bungee cord to keep it closed and tamper-free. That is how lovingly devoted Brooklyn is to her parents. She wants to be with them at all times.

This beautiful girl is so needy she will do anything for affection, and I mean anything. This past Halloween, when her mom took down the decorations, she absentmindedly put the five-foot scarecrow in her office. Much to her amusement, she kept finding Brooklyn quietly sitting in front of the scarecrow, looking up and pawing at it to pet her. As her mom said, Brooklyn will do anything for attention.

A LOVING FOREVER HOME

Brooklyn loves her two siblings, but she prefers the company of humans who have hands, which means petting, belly rubs, and treats. She's a reasonably low-maintenance girl, as long as she's the center of your attention, even if you're a scarecrow.

CHELSEA

"No animal that I know of can consistently be more of a friend and companion than a dog."
~Stanley Leinwall~

Chelsea, a purebred golden retriever, was adopted by a wonderful family of four. Her journey before the adoption was not a simple straight line. She was retired as a breeding dog after one litter of puppies, and she was sold to a service dog association to train her to work with autistic children. Unfortunately, she didn't succeed as a service dog, but she did succeed in getting the best family ever. They were fostering her when they decided to adopt her, as they couldn't imagine life without her.

She loves both her two-legged brothers and walks with them to school every day. She loves her parents, but she's a mommy's girl inside the house and daddy's girl outside. She loves to share her affections evenly within the household, except for the cat. She plays dead if the cat is in the room and only comes back to life once it has left. Maybe she's trying to prove she also has nine lives.

Chelsea loves other dogs, but she prefers humans. She'll exchange some sniffing at the dog parks with the dogs and watch them run around, but she hangs out with people, nudging them for cuddles. Her natural disposition is gentle and sweet.

Chelsea didn't accomplish her service dog credentials because she has a few peculiarities. Nothing big, just a little apprehension or suspicion when it comes to certain aspects of life, but I think we all feel the same way.

She loves Christmas but does not like the Christmas tree. Therefore, don't expect a holiday card from the family with Chelsea and the kids smiling in front of the tree; that will not happen. She'll be in the room next door, waiting for the madness to be over. She also doesn't like fires in the fireplace or outdoor fires. Furthermore, she does not like candles, which may make birthday parties awkward for the two boys, but they love her unconditionally.

Chelsea does not like loud noises such as large trucks passing her on the street or noisy startling sounds inside her home. A couple of men were working in her home recently after the furnace stopped working. She loved all the attention they were giving her until one of the men broke a piece of Styrofoam in half. Chelsea quickly exited the room, and the man apologized profusely to the family. Of course, Chelsea forgave him and returned for some more attention later.

Even though she's a golden retriever, she does not like the water. When her family had a backyard pool, she would not go for a dip. If she's on the beach, she'll chase a ball for as long as someone will throw it. But don't throw it near the water or you'll find yourself retrieving it.

Overall, Chelsea is the sweetest girl who loves every human she meets. When she's out exploring or walking with her family, she takes great offence when people walk by and don't stop to say hi to her. She'll tilt her head in confusion at the blunder and wonder, "What in the world is happening here?" But get out of her way when the snow arrives. She loves to race around as fast as she can, and to her family's delight, she loves to make dog angels on her back in the snow.

Being a retriever, she loves food, but her favorite foods are popcorn or carrots. Her family usually pops a whole bag of popcorn as a Christmas gift each year, and, of course, she gets some on family-movie nights. Perhaps the boys sneak her a few carrots from their plates during dinner, too, because most kids I know aren't crazy about vegetables.

Dogs like Chelsea don't come around often. She's a low-maintenance girl looking for affection from every human she encounters. She'd even get away with stealing the last can of who-hash. Just don't expect her to cuddle up next to you by the fire or pose for Christmas photos.

FINDING A RESPONSIBLE RESCUE

*"Rescue: It's not just a verb.
It's a promise."*
~unknown~

It is widely believed that Britain launched the first formal rescue organization when they created the Society for the Prevention of Cruelty to Animals (SPCA) around 1824. As the movement flourished, people started to view stray dogs differently and recognize them as potential pets.

Today, the public has a strong understanding of animal welfare, and they have a greater awareness of the plight of homeless dogs. Adopting a pet has become a badge of honour for many individuals and families. Those that adopt often become advocates on behalf of abandoned dogs. I call this "unleashing the paws-itive."

Animal rescue organizations and shelters are supported by quality people. They are big-hearted, hard-working, compassionate individuals who devote their time to save dogs. These individuals sacrifice precious time with their families, spouses, children, pets, and even careers to help dogs find loving homes, and to comfort dogs that may have come from distressing situations.

Most rescue organizations attract ethical individuals with high moral standards who do right by the dog and the public. However, before you choose an organization to volunteer with or adopt from, there are characteristics and qualities you should be looking for within the group. You may want to consider dealing with an organization that is registered as non-profit or has a charitable status.

Shelters and independent rescue organizations are entirely different entities. When I refer to a shelter, it means a permanent structure to house homeless dogs. When I talk about rescue, I refer to groups that rely on private foster homes that temporarily care for their dogs. In parts of the book, I will refer to rescue organizations, which include both shelters and rescue organizations.

SHELTER LIFE

Let me introduce you to shelter life. First and foremost, the dogs are protected from the dangers of roaming the streets, or they have been saved from abusive, negligent situations. Please understand shelter dogs are loved and well looked after at the shelter. Volunteers are devoted to caring for the dogs, so much so that, when a winter storm is pending, volunteers will most likely sleep at the shelter to ensure the dogs are protected and feel safe. Volunteers can also become very attached to the dogs and will often have significant input on who will qualify as accepted adopters.

Shelter life can be challenging and busy for volunteers who tend to dogs during the day and well into the night. Dogs must be fed, socialized, and walked, and kennels must be cleaned, among countless other dog care responsibilities. Volunteers and staff must manage each unique dog's necessities and desires. In addition to the animal responsibilities, shelters must also deal with the public.

Life in a shelter can be strenuous and emotionally draining for volunteers, who also help the public with applications during each dog's adoption or surrender. Volunteers check references, answer the never-ending ringing phone, and somebody must handle the impromptu public drop-ins with a pleasant and understanding demeanor.

RESCUE LIFE

Rescue life is just as busy as shelter life. Private rescue organizations work with a network of pre-approved, experienced foster homes. These foster homes provide temporary refuge for the dogs, which means the families safeguard, love, feed, train, and get to know the dog in their private residence. The foster dog becomes part of their family's everyday routine.

Every foster home is assigned a dog that is a good fit for the foster lifestyle. For example, if a surrendered dog does not like other pets, that dog will go to a foster home without pets. The temporary foster home will also fit the dog's energy level, exercise, needs, and individual personality. A great rescue will never use the same foster home continuously. Great rescues will ensure the family takes a well-deserved break between dogs, so they don't burn out. Foster homes are the lifeline and backbone for any rescue to succeed, so the organizations nurture their foster family relationships.

Working alongside foster families are volunteers who pick up surrendered dogs and deliver them to foster care or veterinary appointments. Transportation volunteers are also indispensable for a rescue to survive, and most of the time the volunteers use their private vehicles.

HOW TO FIND A RESPONSIBLE RESCUE ORGANIZATION

Whether the volunteers work with a shelter or rescue organization, they are all devoted to caring for the homeless dogs in their care and ensuring the success of both organizations. Understanding the difference between a shelter and a private rescue organization is essential, but I want to emphasize and highlight what to look for in any responsible animal rescue organization.

IT'S NOT ABOUT SPEED

Most importantly, you want to work with an organization that does not treat the rescue process like a race. The organization must take their time to get to know the dog and uncover what kind of home environment would be best suited for the individual dogs. Setting the dog up for success is the ultimate goal, not how quickly the dog passes through the organization or the number of dogs they rehome. Rescue is not a Formula 1 race or a popularity contest.

MEDICAL CARE

You want an organization that takes every dog in their care to a veterinarian for a health check. The health check is vital as it may discover if the dog has any underlying health issues. This allows the organization to take care of the dog's medical needs before adoption. The organization should also be responsible for spaying or neutering the dog and ensuring the dogs have their first vaccinations.

FUNDRAISING

You should look for an organization that does fundraising all year long, not just on an emergency basis (although emergencies do happen). Fundraising throughout the year is essential for an organization to succeed at daily lifesaving work.

The adoption fee paid by an adopter does not, by any stretch, cover all medical or care expenses, so fundraising all year long is essential. The adoption fee is a nominal fee paid to the rescue organization, and it assists the next dog that lands in their care. It takes a lot of money to save a rescue dog, and the adoption fee is a bargain when you compare it to how much breeders charge when you purchase a dog.

RETAIL RESCUE

An example of a retail rescue is an organization that collects dogs from high-kill shelters and approves the dogs for adoption long before the organization—or most importantly, the adopter—has even met the dog. A responsible rescue will keep the dog from a high-kill shelter in foster care until the organization knows and understands the dog. Only then should they accept applications and place them in a forever home.

In addition, retail rescues invest little to no money in their dogs. If the dog has been spayed, neutered, and even vaccinated by a shelter, the retail rescue does not have to cover those costs. In addition, the retail rescue will have no fees associated with fostering the dog, such as food, bedding, toys, leashes, or training. This is what makes them a "retail" rescue, and the adoption fee goes directly to the organization's bottom line.

The second type of retail rescue deals exclusively with puppies. They may refer to themselves as having "Oops or Accidental" litters. They likely have access to a few female breeding dogs, giving the retailer a constant stream of puppies to sell. These pups may come with their first vaccinations, but the buyer will usually have to pay for spaying or neutering. If you can no longer care for the dog at some point, a retail rescue is unlikely to take the dog back.

"NO-KILL" DESIGNATION

Many years ago, shelters euthanized dogs to create space for new dogs. A friend explained it to me as throwing out the milk. Imagine you came home from grocery shopping and are putting the groceries away. You open your fridge to put the new milk on the shelf. You realize there isn't any room, so you pour out what's left of the old milk to make room for the new jug of milk. That is how some animal shelters worked in the past; they would euthanize dogs to make room for more dogs. It was an old-fashioned, antiquated formula for running a shelter. Thankfully, most shelters no longer operate by those old standards, and the new formula should be credited to Nathan J. Winograd. He is the author of *Redemption: The Myth of Pet Overpopulation and the No Kill Revolution in America*. With time, commitment, and education, Winograd influenced an innovative movement for North American shelters to evolve into no-kill shelters. His solution to reduce or eliminate killing shelter animals was a success and gained a strong following. I would strongly recommend you read his powerful book. Winograd's formula included responsible pet ownership, asking the right questions when a dog is surrendered, among many other innovative ideas. Most shelters and rescues now have a no-kill designation or policy, which may mean they only euthanize in cases involving medical distress or public safety. They do not euthanize to create space for dogs. Please ensure that the organization you deal with has a no-kill philosophy.

PALLIATIVE CARE PROGRAM

Present-day shelters and rescues will most likely have a leading-edge palliative care program. This program ensures that a sick dog who still has time and energy lives out their limited life with an approved palliative foster family. The rescue organization covers the palliative dog's medical expenses.

Dogs in the program may come from an owner who does not want to cover or cannot afford medical costs. Or, the organization may have innocently discovered the dog was ill during its time in foster care. Palliative programs are an integral part of most organizations' accepted platforms.

READ THE ADOPTION APPLICATION

Read an organization's adoption application carefully, as it will include critical information about the group. You should look for items such as whether the organization accepts lifetime responsibility for the dog should you not be able to care for it in the future. It may state that the dog must live inside your home, how long they feel the dog can be left alone daily, and that the dog is never to be tethered outside 24/7. You should ask if the organization is registered, and they should be asking for extensive references from their potential adopters. They may offer an estimate of the annual cost of caring for the dog. Lastly, they may list acceptable dog training methods, and the contract may stipulate that prong, shock, or electric collars or electrical fencing may not be used as training or containing devices.

DO NOT ADOPT (DNA)

Rescue organizations are not top-secret groups running mysterious missions. There's no magical recipe that works for one or all groups. Their collective goal is to find the perfect loving forever home for one of their dogs. And most will do everything possible to protect the dogs under their care, such as keeping an unofficial DNA list. The names on this unofficial list are usually shared privately among the more established or progressive rescue organizations. It is an unofficial list of known animal abusers (some charged or facing pending charges) and people who have abandoned animals or proven to be horrible animal owners. The unofficial list protects animals in care with rescue organizations. It may not be a formal list, but people who run rescue organizations will privately share names with other rescue organizations, of individuals who should not adopt one of their dogs. I feel a national registry of convicted animal abusers should be created, monitored, updated and made available to the public, as it may help stem the flow of animal abusers.

PETA (PEOPLE FOR THE ETHICAL TREATMENT OF ANIMALS)

I have included PETA in this book because people often ask me if I support the organization. My answer is NO. Most people dedicated to animal advocacy and animal rescue do not support PETA.

You may wonder if PETA has done some good. Yes, but their tactics and methods for getting their messages out tells me everything I need to know about the organization. They use shock tactics in their advertising and messaging which I find radical and in bad taste.

In 2010, they ran ads of people doing everyday things with their dogs, but the dogs are in body bags. Images included a body bag hanging out a car window or someone dragging one down the street. PETA prints across the screen at the end of the video, "If you buy a dog, what will you do with the shelter dog you killed? Adopt. Never buy."

In 2008, they ran anonymous ads in *Dog Fancy* magazine, "Just bought a brand-new purebred puppy? Welcome him or her into your home with a free gift bag! Call us today at 1-866-834-6061." When people called the number, they discovered the gift bag was a body bag for the shelter dog PETA claims you killed.

ALL BREED & BREED SPECIFIC RESCUES

In my experience, most rescues accept any breed, or mixed-breed dogs. That said, there are some organizations dedicated to saving specific breeds of dogs such as Labrador Retrievers, German Shepherds, Beagles, or any other purebred dog. But I also find the breed specific rescues do take in mixed breed dogs, from time to time.

DO YOUR HOMEWORK

Many responsible rescue organizations and shelters are looking for volunteers, and of course, they have dogs looking for forever homes. Ensure that you ask questions about how the organization operates. You want your volunteer efforts or donated funds to go to an ethical, credible organization, and you want to know how the dogs in their care are looked after.

"Only do what your heart tells you."
~Princess Diana~

WALLY

*"Every snack you make, every meal you bake,
every bite you take...I'll be watching you."*
~unknown~

Wally is a handsome, silly, five-year-old Biewer Terrier-mix rescue dog adopted through a responsible rescue organization. He was two years old when he arrived, after being surrendered by a family who didn't want him. The organization that saved him is an accountable and responsible group that had one of their dedicated fosters pick him up. His foster mom adopted him, and she said she knew he wasn't leaving her home when she met him.

During his foster care, it was discovered that Wally was quite ill, and the group spared no expense to help him get better, but first they had to find out what was making him so sick. Wally spent three days in a veterinary hospital undergoing many tests such as CT scans, blood work, and many examinations. While at the hospital, one veterinarian contacted the group as he wanted to adopt little Wally. People fall in love with this guy as soon as they meet him because he's got that Hollywood-cool thing happening, just like Ryan Reynolds.

While he was in the hospital, it was discovered that Wally had a liver shunt. A liver shunt causes problems with the blood vessels entering the liver. The blood vessels transport blood through the liver to filter the blood to remove wastes, medications, and toxins from the body and absorb nutrients from the food. If the blood vessels skip the liver, these things do not occur, and you have a very sick dog. Your dog may present a few of the following symptoms if it has a liver shunt: seizures, vomiting, excessive thirst, and stumbling.

Wally went home to the foster for ten days before his surgery as he needed to be put on an anti-seizure medicine beforehand. The surgery was successful, and Wally is living his best life ever, and he will tell you that himself.

Wally loves to garden, and anything in the garden is fair game. He'll drag a cucumber that is bigger than he is to chew on. Strawberries, beans, and carrots are easy for him to steal and devour. He's a clever little man who doesn't let his size get in the way of his fun.

Wally loves to go on ten-kilometer hikes with his mom. He can keep up with, and run under, the big dogs. He's a frequent guest at most local fundraisers, and everyone wants to have their picture taken with him. He is bright, entertaining, food motivated, and loves all other animals, especially his two big dog brothers. Wally can do dog agility, and he even took a dance class with his mom. Wally is a great dancer, even though he has two left feet.

This little guy has an exuberant and loving personality, and he owes his life to the rescue organization, which spared no expense to save his life. He repays their kindness by attending every fundraiser he possibly can, and he raises money in his photo kissing booth. Who wouldn't want to kiss that sweet face?

BADGER

"Opening up your life to a dog who needs a home is one of the most fulfilling things you can do."
~Emma Kenney~

As far as I know, there isn't a barometer to measure how much someone loves their dog. But in Badger's case, I think his dad broke that mythical barometer entirely. I booked a phone call with Badger's dad, and he called me right on time. I didn't know that Badger's dad was in the hospital. When he told me, I quickly suggested that we talk some other time, but he insisted on sharing Badger's story from his hospital bed. I'd say that act alone speaks volumes about the character of the person and his bond with his dog.

Badger's close-knit family of four adopted him when he was a tiny puppy. A tiny puppy who, in two years, grew into seventy-six pounds of shedding fun. Badger spends a day or two each week going to doggy daycare, where he races around and begs every dog to play with him. If a dog isn't participating in the fun, Badger will lean into the dog with his nose to entice them to join, which most do because Badger is the party animal at daycare. They should refer to Badger as "Fifty Shades of Play." He's also the most popular boy at local dog parks, where he hangs out with his buds, and they chase each other nonstop.

When not in doggy daycare, Badger goes to City Hall with his dad. He even has a couple of beds, a makeshift office, a water bowl, marrow bones, and plenty of treats to keep him busy when dad is working. Badger has also figured out which desks at City Hall have the highest quality treats, and he's not shy about asking for a few. At least Badger isn't asking for a government handout, and he is not on the payroll just yet.

Badger's dad is also a business professor at a local university, and his mom is the owner-operator of two daycare centers. Badger can't go to university because the students would never get their work done with this rambunctious boy running around the classroom, and he cannot visit the daycare centers because he'd eat all the kids' treats and then expect them to give him all their attention.

Badger has a love affair with food, and he acts as though he's hungry twenty-four hours a day. If he even suspects there may be food in your hand, he'll turn himself inside out with his clowning, just for a chance to grab that little morsel of food. He will sit, spin, offer his paw, or lie down without anyone asking, just at the thought of a treat. You'd think a very food-motivated dog would be easy to train, but not Badger. The boy is way too social and friendly to pay attention to his owners because he may have to meet that person who is two blocks away.

Besides being a social butterfly, Badger is genuinely the perfect pet, aside from his one fashion hang-up: he dislikes construction workers or school crossing guards who wear reflective orange vests. He comically loses his mind when he sees them—every time. He genuinely believes orange is not the new black. His family should get Calvin Klein or Ralph Lauren on the phone. Badger has an opinion about fashion that he needs to get off his chest.

Badger also has a bit of a foot fetish. He carries his family's shoes to his bed—not to chew them, but to arrange them so he can sleep with them. Let's hope his family doesn't own Manolo Blahniks or Jimmy Choos, as that could become an expensive infatuation.

For such a rambunctious boy, he's uncharacteristically gentle with his squeaky stuffed toys. He'll carry them around for weeks and even months, but if he sees a tiny bit of stuffing coming out, it's game over. Once, his granny fixed his stuffed alligator. It was his prized possession, and when the belly had a tiny rip, she patched it up; Badger refused to play with it ever again.

Badger's family loves the outdoors, and they go camping as often as they can. This includes adventures like sleeping in tents, eating outdoors, swimming, and kayaking. Badger loves it all, and he doesn't mind water as long as his feet can touch the bottom. The silly boy loves kayaking; he tries to grab the water lilies floating by, often upsetting the kayak.

Badger had a favorite upholstered chair as a puppy, which he claimed as his own. Even though he's fully grown now, he can still wriggle himself into the tight-fitting chair, just like a performer from Cirque du Soleil. He has beds all over his house, but he loves his chair. He also whines when the unthinkable happens; someone else sits in his chair!

Badger loves his family, and they also love him dearly. He's more than a pet; he's a treasured family member and will be for all of his life.

SILVER

"The world would be a nicer place if everyone had the ability to love as unconditionally as a dog."
~M. K. Clinton~

Silver is a magnificent pure white husky-mix boy. Whatever he's mixed with, he got all the best features, making it impossible to take a bad picture of him. His faithful dad doesn't care what breed or mixed-breed Silver is because he loves his fifteen-plus-year-old boy unconditionally.

Silver landed in his dad's home as a foster dog about six and a half years ago. Silver was very fortunate to find such a big-hearted foster dad who had extensive experience fostering many dogs. This foster dad was also well aware of the dangers of falling in love with a foster dog. He cares for his foster dogs as if the dog was recently born. He does this because some foster dogs come without a past. They may have been found wandering, lost, or almost feral. So his mission as a foster dad is getting to know the dog's true personality, and he does this with great love and humor. This funny foster dad has a background in film, including movies, television, and commercials. He also hilariously documents his conversations with Silver on social media. As an example:

"Silver's nail trimming appointment was cancelled today because the vet said they don't have enough techs on staff to control him when he gets angry. I know I should be embarrassed, but I'm impressed that even in his senior years (15+), he's still a badass! I imagine it's how you feel when you hear grandpa got kicked out of the nursing home for beating up three orderlies for trying to remove the still he built in his room!"

Silver gives him plenty of material to write about:

"Yes, pop. I know that it's raining out. And that it's very windy. And that the roads and sidewalks are hazardous. But you still haven't explained to me why we can't go to the dog park!"

And even more comical flair:

"Silver needs to go out. I have no choice but to walk him in the thunder and lightning (and rain)! If this is my last post, I've had a good life!"

As a foster dog, Silver came with a doggy kerchief that read "Adoptable" on one side and "Adopted" on the other. The rescue organization called the funny foster dad about a month after Silver moved in. The organization had a family that was very interested in adopting Silver. The foster dad thought long and hard about parting with Silver, and he couldn't let the boy go. They had formed a deep emotional bond, and they were very content living together. He also worried no other dog would ever understand his jokes. The rescue organization congratulated him and jokingly told him to turn the scarf over to read "Adopted," and he did just that.

Silver and his dad have a very happy, content life together. With his dad working from home more often, they get to share their meals. Silver will leave the kibble in his bowl for hours, just in case his dad plans to eat something a little more interesting. Silver expects all house food to be shared or tested with the husky. Luckily, his dad is a softy and gives in to Silver's every whim or desire.

Like every other dog on this planet, Silver has a couple of quirks. He must, at all times, walk through the door or up the stairs in front of his dad. God forbid his dad is hurried and goes first, Silver will stoically stand in place until his dad remembers and returns to the starting point. Then, and only then, will Silver become Quicksilver and continue to walk.

Over the years, Silver has jumped into bed with his dad. This only lasts for a few minutes, as Silver is confused about why he can't have the whole bed to himself. He'll jump down and wander around and usually sleep on the couch. But it's fair game if his dad gets out of bed in the middle of the night.

Even though Silver is now a senior boy, it doesn't stop him and his dad from going for long walks or hikes. Silver has a small cataract in one eye, but he can still spot every duck, squirrel, or bird in his sight. His hearing has diminished, but his dad refers to this as selective hearing. Silver may not always respond to his name, but try opening a bag of chips or a cheese slice, and Silver is beside him in a split second.

Silver is an easy-going dude who loves life, people, and dogs, but he idolizes his dad the most. His dad has repeatedly said that Silver is the best rescue dog he has ever adopted. But don't try to trim his nails; he turns into the Tasmanian devil.

THE THREE MUSKETEERS

"Nobody's going to tell me that my dog doesn't love me. That's crazy talk."
~Carrie Underwood~

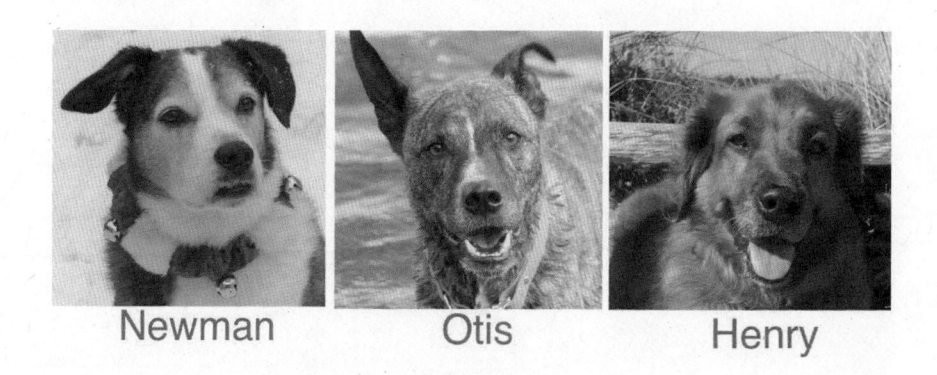

Newman   Otis   Henry

A lovely hard-working married couple who owned and operated a large printing business often talked about getting a small dog someday. But, quite often in the world of dog rescue, a homeless dog will find you.

One cold winter day, a courier arrived at their store and told them he found a puppy in the parking lot. So the couple decided to take the frozen pup to a veterinary clinic. They hoped the pup was microchipped so they could return the puppy to its owner; however, that was not the case. They made posters and hung them everywhere, but the owners never came forward. Looking like a five-year-old child on Christmas day, the wife asked her husband, "Can I keep him?" And they did, for thirteen wonderful years.

Newman was probably a Husky/Shepherd mix who grew into an adorable dog, but he was anything but small. He went to work with his parents every day, and he never complained he wasn't paid a salary. He was paid with treats and affection. He was such a laid-back boy; anytime they went

FINDING A RESPONSIBLE RESCUE

away on vacation, every one of their friends, colleagues, and family members wanted to take care of him. He was just that kind of dog; everyone fell in love with Newman.

Newman was such an old soul that female patrons could not help but kiss his sweet face. This often meant Newman had pink and red lipstick kiss marks on his fur. Of course, Newman was always up for affection and never complained.

When Newman was ten years old, the couple heard about a dog looking for a new home. Even though Newman did not come from a rescue organization, he opened the door for two other dogs. They met Otis, fell in love, and brought him home. Newman was such an easy-going dog, he warmly accepted Otis into his home. But Otis was full of mischief, and he tormented the older man daily. If Otis was awake, Newman wouldn't get any rest, but he took it all in stride. Otis would hang off Newman's ears, eat his food, grab all of the toys, lie on top of him, and be a pain in the butt. But Newman was perfect, and he never complained.

Newman even allowed Otis to come to work every day. If Otis was being a nuisance at the office, his mom would put him in the time-out room, which was hilarious for people coming and going from the business because the time-out room had a big window. Otis would look out the window and perform silly stunts to make people laugh. People who didn't even have business to transact would enter to tell the couple what Otis was up to. Some children even asked, "Is there something wrong with your dog, and is he defective?" Kids were bewildered by Otis's look of one ear up and one ear down.

When Newman crossed the bridge, Otis and his parents were heartbroken. After a while, when their tears dried and their hearts started to heal, they adopted handsome Henry. Otis quickly learned karma because Henry tormented him like he had annoyed old Newman. I guess that is what they mean by "what goes around, comes around."

Henry is so handsome that his mom often says he's just getting by on his looks. Henry of course goes to work with Otis, and they are the official greeters at the counter when clients are picking up their print orders. They also sit and stare at everything coming off the printing press. I assume they are quality control for the business.

RECYCLED LOVE

As Otis is getting older, Henry will wait for hours each weekend at home for someone to play with him. He loves chasing a ball and hates being groomed. To agree to grooming, he must have a ball in his mouth.

Newman, Otis, and Henry are three incredible rescue dogs who were very fortunate to have such a loving home. They thrived on being part of a wonderful family, and they lavished their parents with affection. They were also pleased to have rewarding careers as official greeters. Life doesn't get much better than that.

SADIE

"Our prime purpose in this life is to help others. And if you can't help them, at least don't hurt them."
~Dalai Lama~

Sadie was adopted when she was one year old. She's a Cavalier King Charles Spaniel who should be on a greeting card. She's a natural beauty—simply gorgeous. If she were a Hollywood actress, Natalie Portman and Angelina Jolie would be losing acting roles to Sadie.

Sadie had a rough start in life. She was born in a dreadful puppy mill and promptly sold. Dogs born in large-scale breeding facilities can suffer from stress and anxiety, which was the case with Sadie. She was terrified of everything, so the people who bought her returned her to the mass breeding establishment. The proprietor took her to a veterinary clinic to be euthanized. Luckily, the veterinarian had a close relationship with a local rescue organization and Sadie was saved.

The young couple that adopted Sadie fell head over heels in love with the sweet girl. When they first brought her home, they kept a harness on her, making it easier for them and quicker for Sadie to hook on a leash. Sadie showed no aggression or reactive behavior towards her new parents, but she was still fearful. She slowly started warming up to her dad before her mom. But mom finally won her over.

They could not make eye contact with Sadie because Sadie liked to make herself invisible to everyone. One day her mom closed off the living room and stayed in the room with her. Each time her mom got up, she moved a foot closer to little Sadie. When she was finally within reach of petting Sadie's face, she did so, and Sadie melted. She got up on the couch and fell into her mom's lap. Sadie cuddled with her and placed her little head on her mom's chest, where she spends all her time now. Her mom became her security blanket.

Her mom leaves some of her old clothing lying around the house to ensure Sadie is comfortable. She does this because Sadie has developed a habit of chewing on her clothing, and she leaves tiny holes in the clothing. Her mom doesn't mind as long as Sadie is happy. Her mom and dad also realize Sadie is not a girl who plays with toys, so the clothing is essential to keep her engaged.

Sadie is a sweet girl who lures people in with her Bambi-like eyes, then barks at them. She truly trusts only three people in her world: mom, dad, and the dear friend who watches her when her parents are away.

FINDING A RESPONSIBLE RESCUE

Sadie loves food, but surprisingly her favorite is bananas. She also loves car rides, so her parents sometimes take her for a spin around the neighborhood, even if they don't have plans to go anywhere. Her mom posted a video last year of Sadie sitting on the front passenger seat with the air conditioning blowing on her. I thought she looked like Shania Twain singing, "I Feel Like a Woman." It was adorable.

As beautiful and sweet as little Sadie is, she has developed some genetic problems. She has ulcers in her throat and has acid reflux. She's on pain medication for both issues. But her most significant issue is her back. She has compressed discs, and she's having a minor mobility issue with the condition. Her parents take her to a clinic for acupuncture and chiropractic adjustments. If she needs surgery in the future, her parents will ensure it is done right away. They will do everything possible to secure Sadie's health and happiness.

Fun fact: Sadie's mom owns and operates a business called The Dog Shop—take a wild guess whose sweet face is the logo for the company. If you guessed Sadie, you're right.

Although Sadie had a hard, bumpy start in life, she certainly won the best parents and fur siblings she could ever have wished for. Sadie is a terrific example of how necessary it is to have veterinary clinics that work closely with rescue organizations. Sadly, if puppy Sadie had been taken to the wrong clinic, she would not be here today. She's the poster dog for how a responsible rescue organization works. She's also a prime example of why rescues need more veterinary clinics to work closely and intimately with them.

Sadie's parents own three rescue dogs, and they hold many fundraising events at The Dog Shop. Little Sadie often attends to make sure everyone participates in helping rescue dogs just like her. If you help out, she may even share one of her bananas with you.

ADOPTING A SPECIAL NEEDS DOG

*"Rescue does not mean 'damaged',
It means they have been let down by humans."*
~unknown~

I believe rescue dogs are not damaged, but the reality is that some dogs will arrive in rescue harmed or wounded from mistreatment, or with abnormalities due to irresponsible breeding. When these dogs arrive, they receive the best medical care possible to help restore their health. With the support of volunteers and foster families, the dogs are given medical or psychological help to assist them in adjusting and moving forward. People involved in rescue have a natural affinity for animals, which guides them to instinctively protect special needs dogs.

I have owned many cherished dogs in my lifetime, and I have also met many wonderful dogs with extraordinary owners. But the dogs that tear my soul to pieces are the special needs dogs. These dogs may have three legs, some are blind or deaf, and others arrive with wheels because they are immobile.

As heartbroken as I feel when I meet them, they restore my faith in humanity because I see how much love and affection their owners lavish on them, and because they provide a safe home where their dogs can thrive. These dog owners will defend their dog when a person looks down on their dog or makes derogatory comments. It is upsetting for dog owners to listen to these remarks because living with a disabled dog is not much different than living with an ordinary dog. Many of these dogs live long lives and bring joy and happiness to their owners.

All dogs have individual or unique needs. For example, if you have a dog obsessed with barking at people when they walk by your house, you need to limit access to the window. If you have a dog with severe separation anxiety, you need to alter your schedule around your dog's fears. This is no different than living with a dog that has physical challenges.

Challenges that come with owning a blind dog are easy to manage once the dog knows the configuration of your home. A deaf dog may need to learn hand signals to keep them safe. Dogs with three legs easily navigate the world around them, but more slowly. Dogs that need wheels to move them through life need more space in the house. Just because a dog is disabled does not mean it can't live a long, happy life. There is plenty of life and love in a disabled dog.

"True love is seen in the eyes of a rescued dog."
~unknown~

ROSIE

"Kindness is the language which the deaf can hear and the blind can see."
~Unknown~

Beautiful, happy, rambunctious, energetic Rosie, an amstaff mixed girl, is living her best life. Rosie does not let the fact that she is deaf slow her down; she breaks those boundaries with lightning speed.

This gorgeous girl made her way to rescue after living in a few unfortunate homes. Luckily, she landed in a great foster home, where she learned how to be a dog. Eventually, a wonderful family adopted her after friends shared Rosie's story. They spoke to the foster mom and made arrangements to meet with Rosie. At the first meeting, Rosie rolled over for a belly rub, and her sweet and loving disposition captured them. The rest was history. They instinctively knew Rosie was a match for their family—maybe even a match made in heaven.

ADOPTING A SPECIAL NEEDS DOG

Rosie is outgoing and enthusiastic about everything, and she loves people, dogs, and bunnies. She may chase bunnies occasionally, but it's all in good fun. She only wants to be everyone's best friend. She loves hiking and the beach. She'll swim as long as her feet can touch the bottom. She doesn't like to stop when hiking because stopping is a waste of time; she has too much to explore. Rosie will go anywhere and do anything fun because she's a party girl at heart. She also has two full-time jobs: de-stuffing toys and enticing humans or dogs to chase her. If only the bunnies would chase her, she'd be so happy.

After they adopted her, Rosie's devoted and faithful parents took her to obedience classes. They taught Rosie hand signals: thumbs up mean good dog, palm up means to sit, stop sign tells her to stay, and a finger wiggle tells her to come to them. If Rosie is turned away from them at home, they lightly stomp the floor, and Rosie will turn around immediately because she doesn't want to miss out on anything. She's a brilliant girl who loves to please her parents and make them laugh with her silly antics. Rosie is also obsessed with cuddling, so be careful when sitting on her couch; this girl will be all over you. She also insists on sleeping with her parents every night, and they do not mind one bit.

Her dad says having Rosie is mutually beneficial, as she gets her parents out exploring the trails, bluffs, and woods. They put a small bell on her collar so they know where she is at all times, but she honestly doesn't travel far from them. If she gets ahead of them on walks, she will stop and turn around to check that her parents are close behind; then she continues exploring.

Her "deaf-defying" actions have been caught many times on camera. One video shows her flying through her house at breakneck speed, launching herself off one sofa, over the coffee table and elegantly landing on the couch across the room, with her favorite toy still in her mouth. There are videos of her running through the woods and circling back to run around her parents, who can never catch her. She even catapulted herself across a stream, so she wouldn't get her feet wet.

While exploring and hiking, Rosie will run—she loves to run—and nothing can slow her down when she's got her speed up. Her parents lovingly refer to her as Rosie-Wrecking-Ball because she's knocked her father over a few times.

Her father is active on social media, documenting her hilarious antics. You can follow Rosie on Instagram: @rosie_an_my_hoomans. People don't realize she's deaf even though she's wearing a collar and vest with the word 'deaf' embroidered on the sides. She's such a social and friendly girl; it's difficult to realize she doesn't hear a word you're saying. Rosie goes about her business, discovering the world and hoping she'll get chased as soon as possible.

Rosie is a valued member in a very loving home with a family that will do everything possible to keep her safe, happy, and content. I could say they'd move mountains for her, but Rosie would beat them to it.

WINNIE AND NASH

"If you have one friend who would sit and wait for you without knowing whether you would come back it's your dog. Cherish that love."
~unknown~

Winnie and Nash are rescue dogs who live with the same wonderful family. The dogs are incredibly close—joined at the hip, some might say. This intimate bond may be the consequence of Winnie being deaf. She follows Nash everywhere and copies everything he does. It is a good thing Nash is such a good boy because he has taught Winnie how to be the best dog possible. The dogs have such a strong bond the family should make a "dog-umentary" called "When Hairy Met Sally."

Winnie and Nash's family of four are very busy. Both children are in university; their mother is busy with the family farm and very involved in dog rescue. Their father is an active politician who, when running his election campaign, took the dogs on the campaign trail. Not many politicians would do that, but when you have terrific dogs like Winnie and Nash, how could he resist?

Volunteers fell in love with the dogs and their funny antics on the campaign trail. One afternoon, much to his delight, Nash quickly polished off a couple of pieces of pizza. Winnie is too much of a lady to partake in that kind of indulgence, but she loves riding in the big bus.

A family initially surrendered Nash, and his foster family gave him a temporary home. But Nash fit in perfectly with the household, and they made him a permanent member of their family. They had to because the boy had turned into a big lap dog.

Winnie was surrendered as a special needs dog by a breeder. He did not sell her, he only wanted to find her a permanent loving home, and he did just that. Winnie's mom refers to her as a specialty-abled dog, not disabled.

Winnie is a Velcro dog and has the typical Border Collie personality; she always wants to play. If she wants you to throw the ball, she'll gently drop it on your lap so you don't miss it. She can be timid when meeting new people, but she warms up if you give her a little space and time.

Both Nash and Winnie know sign language, so when the family signs to Winnie, Nash is often the one that answers. It's easy to forget you have a deaf dog when you're so used to talking to a family pet. So if you tell Winnie she's a good girl, Nash will come running as if you told him he's a good boy, which he is.

When Winnie and her mom are out for walks, Winnie will frequently turn around to check-in. She's incredibly bright and affectionate, and she doesn't like her humans or her treats to be very far away.

Settling Winnie into her forever home took patience, love, and time. She was almost like a feral dog because she had lived on a hundred-acre farm running with other dogs at the breeder's residence. She left her pack situation and moved in with her new family. To help Winnie settle into her new environment, her mom put a leash on her collar and tied it to her belt around her waist, even when they were sleeping. Eventually, once she had her bearings and was more confident, Winnie graduated to dragging the leash around the house.

If Winnie's mom has one message about living with a deaf dog, it is, "You can do it." She finds it incredibly rewarding to see where Winnie is today and how far she has come. She's a lovely dog who wants to be loved, and she has the best fur brother in Nash, her protector.

Some people in politics will tell you just about anything to win an election, but not this rescue dad. He and his wife have fostered and advocated for homeless dogs for more years than they can count. They have raised two incredible young adults who are also animal lovers.

He and his wife understand owning a dog has been proven to be beneficial to one's mental health: blood pressure is lowered when petting a dog; living with a dog can take away loneliness and help with depression; and people receive boundless love from a dog. All this, plus dogs get people outside and can even make people more social. This is why they took the dogs on the campaign trail. They love everyone and were great company on and off the bus.

Both Winnie and Nash live a charmed life, and they share much love and happiness with their family. All rescue dogs should be as lucky as to find a loving, supportive home. They can be found lounging on the couch or running around on the farm. And don't worry, Winnie will also come running if you call for Nash.

JEB

*"The one thing we can never get enough of is love.
And the one thing we never give enough of is love."*
~Henry Miller~

Jeb is a five-year-old purebred Blue Heeler (Australian Cattle Dog). The breed is used as a herding dog for cattle as their breed supposedly thrives and flourishes when they have a job. But Jeb didn't get the memo, and no one told him. He'd rather chase a ball, eat everything in your kitchen, and sleep on the couch. He's a happy-go-lucky boy who doesn't let his disability slow him down; Jeb is deaf. When his breeder discovered this, he made an appointment to have Jeb euthanized. By a stroke of luck, a woman saved Jeb and surrendered him to an incredible rescue organization. And that is where his life cheerfully began.

The woman who governs and operates the rescue organization agreed to take puppy Jeb. This intake was unfolding while her cousin was visiting, so the cousin jumped at the chance to foster the little deaf puppy. Since then,

ADOPTING A SPECIAL NEEDS DOG

Jeb has never left her house, and that was five years ago. Jeb's mom works in the educational system, working with special needs children. She must have wings, because Jeb is not the only dog she has fostered for her cousin. Her home has been opened up to homeless dogs many times, but Jeb is the only one she couldn't bear to part with.

Jeb is a social boy who used to go to doggy daycare. Now he stays home, sleeps on the couch, and never takes his eyes off his mom. He also attends as many rescue fundraisers as possible. He quickly learned fundraisers have the best treats. His mom refers to him as her spoiled boy who loves life. She also said a ball is his best friend and he'd play fetch twenty-four hours a day if he could.

Jeb is a brilliant boy, which made training him that much easier. His mom taught him a few hand signals resulting in Jed knowing how to sit, stay, come, no, yes, and no barking. Outside of Jeb's sweet, calm disposition, you will never find him watching The Tour de France. Bicycles are his weakness, just like kryptonite is to Superman. Jeb gets startled when a bike races past him; he can't herd or steer the bike into his pack. Jeb's slogan is, "Say no to bikes."

But Jeb loves car rides. He sits in the front seat, often on the armrest, and he is his mom's favorite co-pilot. He's spoiled rotten when they go to a drive-thru as the "window people" always make a big deal when they see Jeb's sweet face. Of course, Jeb always welcomes treats, praise, and petting.

Some dogs are food-motivated, but Jeb takes it to the next level. Food is his obsession. He loves everything, so he is not a picky eater, and he loses his mind for blueberries or watermelon. His mom makes him a unique frozen yogurt/blueberry treat that is Jeb's favorite delicacy. She even puts the concoction in a Kong and keeps a supply of them in the freezer. But Jeb is not spoiled; well, maybe he is, and that's just fine with his mom.

This comical, entertaining boy has one funny habit that leaves people cracking up; Jeb loves to smile. Not just a slight grin, it's a full-on, roll back his lips and show all his teeth smile. When friends come to visit, they will ask Jeb to smile, so he smiles and relishes the attention they lavish on him. For a little deaf boy, he truly knows how to communicate and please people.

Jeb lives near the ocean, but he's not a water-loving dog. He will lie down in the water to cool off on a hot day, but he doesn't go in over his head unless his mom is swimming. That is the only time he'll venture out and swim because his mom is his whole world.

This little guy is living a fulfilling and rewarding life. If you ever get a chance to meet him, don't bring your bike because that won't make him smile. Bring blueberries.

TUCKER

"It's not how much we give but how much love we put into giving."
~Mother Teresa~

This stunning one-year-old boy's name is Tucker. He's a mix of Standard Poodle and Catahoula Leopard Dog. As you can see in the picture, he has wheels, and he loves to be on the move, so he often needs his tires replaced.

Tucker came from a breeder. At five weeks old, a barn door crushed his lower back. He eventually landed in the arms of two dedicated rescuers who fostered the little guy. They showered him with affection and lovingly exercised his back legs with guidance from a devoted veterinarian. When Tucker was more robust and ready to move on, the rescue organization that saved him found him the best possible home, and this boy is dearly loved.

His mom told me that Tucker doesn't even notice that he can't walk. She said, "He's utterly oblivious to his circumstances." And she credits the rescue organization and fosters that treated him like a regular dog. Tucker's mom now volunteers with the same organization to thank them for everything they did to help support her remarkable dog.

Adopting a homeless dog seems to open your heart, and this family is all heart. They even have rescue roosters and chickens that live in a heated, warm coop. Every animal is treated like a cherished family member.

Tucker's mom said she couldn't imagine a life without him. He loves everyone he meets, and in return they also fall in love with Tucker. He's a happy-go-lucky boy who loves to go for long walks, hiking and running on the beach. He's just a young boy, and he's already grown out of three sets of wheels. The kind-hearted woman who runs the rescue organization said, "Tucker's soon going to need to have his own parking lot."

Owning a dog with wheels certainly works for this family, and they will bend over backward to ensure that he has a happy, rewarding life. They often take off Tucker's wheels to give his hips a break. They place Tucker on a soft memory foam bed when the wheels are off. His mom said he tends to favor one side when he lies down, so she lovingly flips him over to ensure he's comfortable.

Tucker is also a social butterfly and loves other dogs. He lives with two other dogs, but there can often be up to five dogs in the house, which makes him very happy. There is also a black lab who lives down the street, and Tucker is obsessed with him. When he is out for a walk with his mom and they pass the house, Tucker cries because he wants the dog to come out and play with him. Tucker is the perfect dog, and one of his favorite things to do is play tug of war with other dogs. He also loves to greet his dad at the door at the end of each day. Tucker will gently grab his dad's sleeve and guide him to his favorite chair, where he can pet Tucker for as long as possible.

In today's complicated world, with so little good news, it's uplifting to meet a family who is so devoted to a disabled dog. Tucker is supported and surrounded with love. And this family will buy him as many wheels as he can burn through in his lifetime. What dog could ask for anything more?

CANINE COVID CRISIS

"The greatness of a nation and its moral progress can be judged by the way its animals are treated."
~Gandhi~

Two very different themes emerged during the pandemic: you either learned to bake bread or got a puppy. I admit I became one of those bakers while other North American homes exploded with dogs and puppies.

The unprecedented demand for puppies created a severe, adverse effect on animal health and welfare. Far too many North Americans adopted or purchased puppies and dogs during the global crisis, hoping their new addition would alleviate their feelings of isolation, loneliness, and anxiety. Many obtained the dog with good intentions; however, animal advocates became concerned as they witnessed an acute animal crisis develop. Puppies, adolescent dogs, and adult dogs began to arrive in shelters and rescues.

Therefore, the outcome from the crisis is being felt in every rescue organization, shelter, veterinary clinic, and community. Issues such as behavioral problems, serious health concerns, and limited access to critical veterinary care are all challenges caused by the canine Covid crisis, referred to by some as a puppy pandemic. Unfortunately, I believe this crisis will continue long after the pandemic ends.

RESCUES AND SHELTERS

Although animal rescue organizations initially experienced a welcome surge in adoptions during the pandemic, the euphoria was short-lived because pet owners began to surrender their newly-acquired dogs in record numbers. Families who adopted or bought dogs without doing their due diligence started handing them over as they realized the daily obligations of pet ownership were too much. As people went back to office life, took holidays, went to the gym, started socializing, or began enrolling their kids in after-school and weekend activities, they suddenly realized they had no time for the dog.

Shelters and rescues filled up, and with many at capacity, they could no longer take in new dogs. The organizations had to create waitlists for people trying to surrender their dog.

To complicate the issue, rescue organizations and shelters also began to witness behavioral problems with surrendered dogs. These were issues that shelters and rescues did not usually see before the pandemic. Therefore, it took more time to find the dogs new homes and the organizations have incurred additional expenses because they need to hire trainers to help the dogs overcome aggression, separation anxiety, poor house training, or other socialization problems. Sadly, fundraising slowly dried up or came to a complete halt during the pandemic, leaving many organizations on the brink of closing their doors.

The pandemic also created issues in how organizations adopted their dogs out. With lockdowns, home visits stopped and hand-offs for approved adopted dogs were done with great difficulty.

Some rescue organizations were also being burdened with dogs that needed to be euthanized. As a result of the pandemic and rising inflation rates, families could not afford to euthanize their dog at a veterinary clinic, therefore they surrendered the dog.

BEHAVIORAL PROBLEMS

As a result of lockdowns and restrictions, many dogs missed out on the most critical time in their short lives: to become properly socialized. A dog with positive, consistent training will be able to live a well-balanced life. But obedience classes or access to trainers was at an all-time low across North America due to restrictions, leaving new pet owners sitting on waitlists.

First-time dog owners did not understand the daily demands of owning a dog. Nor did they research or seek advice on the breed before purchasing.

Therefore, the dogs were not walked, adequately exercised, or properly socialized. Leaving a dog to its own devices only creates issues for that dog. Many dogs were not taught boundaries, so these dogs became reactive to both other dogs and people. Many dogs were nervous, aggressive, did not like children, or had other social issues.

Puppies need puppy classes to socialize with other dogs, and families learn how to train them during the same classes. They need to be introduced to many new positive experiences to become confident, social family pets. Young dogs need to experience new sights, smells, objects, and people. Otherwise they become fearful of those everyday parts of life. Without early socialization, these pups grow into anxious, worried, stressed dogs. They can develop severe separation anxiety, leading to a lifelong struggle.

Separation anxiety is a terrible state of mind for a dog to live with. They need help to overcome or work through the condition because leaving them to "work it out" does not help the dog. Separation anxiety, along with food or dog aggression, needs assistance and training to overcome this psychological issue.

Adopted adolescent or adult dogs also benefit from obedience classes, as it helps the new family learn how to communicate with the dog. Again, restrictions meant many dogs did not get the early family intervention or assistance required.

SERIOUS HEALTH ISSUES

Many dogs or puppies bought online during the pandemic have had severe health issues. These dogs most likely came from backyard breeders and mass dog farm businesses that are profiting from the increased demand for dogs. We have heard stories about some new dog owners experiencing the death of their new pet only weeks after taking them into their homes. Other dogs are developing cancer or blindness at very young ages. Sadly, other severe health issues such as hip dysplasia or heart murmurs will also develop long after the pandemic and as the dogs mature.

Unbelievably, some people who purchased dogs or pups impulsively are now putting their dogs up for sale to recoup the money they paid to breeders and for veterinary care.

UNSCRUPULOUS BREEDERS

The one group you do not need to pity are the unethical and immoral breeders worldwide who benefited from the pandemic because of the increased demand for dogs. Breeders have significantly increased the price to purchase one of their dogs. Many breeders and dog brokers also imported dogs from foreign large-scale dog farms all over the globe to North America. Many of these animals are unhealthy and were at risk when they were transported. For example, in 2020 a European plane arrived in Canada with 500 crated French bulldog puppies, but 38 dogs died during transport.

These crated puppies coming to North America are often sold online or on social media platforms like Kijiji and Facebook. These sites appear to look like legitimate breeding businesses, but they were not. Some greedy breeders are even sinking to new lows and are posing as rescue organizations. With the demand for dogs during the pandemic, many dogs will be paying the price with their lives or will suffer from lifelong physical and mental health problems. Sadly, the USDA (United States Department of Agriculture) had to inform the public they were limiting their inspections of breeder facilities as a result of the pandemic and concern for their government employees.

There are also many stories about dog thefts, because in some cases breeders could not produce enough dogs to meet the demand—this created an underground puppy trade. For example, Lady Gaga's dogs were stolen, and her dog walker was shot. Authorities believed the dognappers did not know the dogs belonged to the superstar singer. The police believe the dogs were stolen because they were French bulldogs that could fetch the criminals thousands of dollars when resold. The criminals were caught and criminal charges were filed. The dog walker survived, after a lengthy recovery and the dogs were returned to Lady Gaga.

ACCESS TO CRITICAL VETERINARY CARE

As a result of the pandemic, a veterinarian's career has become mentally and emotionally challenging. Protecting the health of our pets has always been their top priority, but because of world circumstances they have had to adjust how they conduct their business.

Clinics had to initiate new processes during lockdowns, such as a closed-door policy. The clinic's front doors were locked, prohibiting the public from entering. Therefore, you had to call the clinic in advance if you needed to fill a prescription or buy pet food or other miscellaneous items. Staff would then greet you outside with your purchase and accept your payment.

The closed-door policy also affected appointments for your pet. You had to call the clinic once you arrived, and a staff member would meet you outside to collect your pet. During the appointment, the veterinarian would call with updates on the diagnosis and suggestions for your pet. The closed-door policy was difficult for veterinarians, clinic staff, pet owners, and the animals.

Overall, pet owners were respectful and thankful for the services of their clinic, especially under the circumstances. However, it was shocking to hear of the increased number of incidents of clients being disrespectful to veterinarians and clinic staff.

With the influx of new pets, many veterinary clinics had to post notices saying that they could no longer take on new clients. And existing clients did not have the quick access to their veterinarian they had in the past.

Formal complaints rose significantly along with online or social media bashing. Most of the complaints were about owners expecting quick access to their veterinarians, but wait times drastically increased with so many new pets. Add to this the fact that many of these dogs were so poorly bred that their health problems required multiple appointments at the clinic instead of the usual one or two annual visits.

In some cases, veterinarians were also forced to deliver heartbreaking news to new pet owners that their dogs would not live long because of serious underlying health issues. Or, sadly, the veterinarian would discover the pet they bought was blind or deaf or would be very soon. As a result, veterinarians and their teams were stretched, and many suffered from compassion fatigue. Sadly, some veterinarians have walked away from the industry while many are suffering from severe mental health problems, contributing to a rise in the number of suicides in the profession.

Veterinarians, on most days, need to be grief councillors, run a business, act as financial advisors, time managers, and human resource officers—and practice medicine. Add a pandemic, keyboard warriors on social media, and the emotional whiplash that happens multiple times a day; veterinarians are challenged. You can't go from vaccinating puppies or kittens straight to euthanasia appointments, or deliver painful news to a pet owner, and think your mental health won't be affected. Life is not easy for veterinarians, and the pandemic added a whole new level of stress, burden, and pressure that will be felt for years to come.

COMMUNITY EFFECTS

Untrained, un-socialized dogs affect communities in many negative ways. These dogs can bite a child or adult, or attack another dog. These dogs can make walking around your neighborhood stressful. It can also pit neighbors against each other and disrupt or change the pulse of a previously calm and peaceful community.

I have witnessed firsthand dogs bought or adopted during the pandemic. I have encountered dogs that are incredibly nervous, or are reactive to both people and other dogs. The anxious dogs look like they want to be anywhere other than on a walk. Their body language is usually the same; tails between their legs, no eye contact, and they dart behind the walker if you get too close. I have encountered a reactive pup wearing a shock collar, with the owner holding the remote. The stories these people share with me are always similar: 1) I bought the dog for the kids as they are doing schoolwork remotely during the lockdown, 2) I am working from home and I wanted company, and 3) This is my first dog, but it's more work than I thought. Unfortunately, my gut tells me these dogs are likely to be surrendered in the next few months, or they may be euthanized.

PET CUSTODY CASES

Lawyers are witnessing a spike in pet custody cases in North America. Covid-19 lockdowns and work-from-home mandates forced couples to spend more time together, and for some it turned out to be too much togetherness. Couples who have decided to separate are hiring lawyers to help decide who gets the pet. These pet custody cases can cost tens of thousands of dollars and can drag on for months or years.

AFTER THE PANDEMIC

Rescue and shelter organizations will continue to receive unwanted pets long after we get back to everyday life. Fundraising may increase, but funding will likely remain complicated, with many households suffering economic hardships during the pandemic and with increased inflation affecting households. Behavior issues caused by poor breeding or training in pandemic dogs will continue to be a significant problem. Unscrupulous breeders will continue to produce unhealthy dogs with genetic defects.

With the rate of new pets added to families during the pandemic, veterinarians will endure the stress in their careers for years to come. Add to the fact that unhealthy dogs will require multiple appointments; therefore, wait times for appointments will continue to increase. And add to the mix: many clinics are no longer taking on new patients. The imbalance will take years to correct—if it can be fixed.

HOW PET OWNERS CAN HELP

If you are looking for a new pet, be smart and be kind. Choose a great preservation breeder so you will be confident you are purchasing a healthy puppy, or adopt from a responsible rescue organization. Support rescues and shelters that keep their dogs and communities safe. By adopting a wonderful homeless dog, you are helping to support organizations. If you can, donate to a local organization. You can donate funds, items, or your valuable time.

Be kind to veterinarians and their staff. Every person working at the clinic loves animals, and that is why they chose the profession. They are under tremendous stress on the best of days. Please be respectful.

DOG STORIES

I have not included rescue stories in this chapter on purpose. The pandemic has been horrible for everyone in North America including rescue dogs. I did not want a beloved rescue dog associated with such a desperate global catastrophe that crushed the world.

TALK DOGGY TO ME

*"Rescue dogs are like snowflakes.
No two are the same."*
~Tracy Jessiman~

I was overwhelmed with the response from rescue dog owners when I approached them to share their stories with me. Not one person declined the opportunity. I was inspired and even enlightened by the passion and joy that resonated from every rescue dog owner. They proudly showcased the deep special bond with their pet, and I was emotionally moved by the tears many shed when sharing their stories about their beloved pet.

I feel dogs have the ability to enrich human lives in every way possible, just as we can improve a rescue dog's life. While both humans and dogs can be starved, beaten, abandoned, abused, or neglected, dogs tend to move forward with greater ease. Many of the dogs in this book came from difficult situations, but they all thrived in their new homes. Can we learn from dogs? YES, I feel we can. Dogs provide the perfect example of living in the moment. I believe anything is possible when it comes to dogs.

People often wonder if dogs feel or sense the same emotions we feel; are they sentient beings? For a dog to be labelled a sentient being, it has to experience emotions such as pain, delight, anxiety, or joy. Is it those shared emotions that attract us to dogs? I am not a scientist, but I have spent most of my life observing dogs. I feel I can say with great confidence that I have witnessed first-hand many different emotions from dogs. Some have been shy, nervous, afraid, happy, and even confident. I've owned dogs who are jealous when I pet another dog or overwhelmed in certain situations. Humans feel these same emotions. Maybe this is why we are so attracted to dogs.

Dogs also provide us with unconditional love, and they unite us, even those of us who have had challenging backgrounds or experiences. If a dog can forget their past and live in the moment, possibly humans can learn to do the same on some small level.

While I was having conversations with the rescue dog owners, I was ill-prepared for the range of emotions during each discussion. The central theme was how much their dog has inspired them and how well the dog is thriving in their home. They talked about all the wonderful things their dog brings to their lives. But most importantly, they explained that they do not regard rescue dogs as damaged.

I repeatedly heard about many beneficial, life-changing experiences people have encountered after rescuing a dog. These dog owners understand that they saved more than a life; they rescued a soul, which may be why rescue dog owners smile a little more often.

Dogs offer unconditional love and devotion to their families. They make people feel less lonely, keep us active, and make us social and more spontaneous. Most importantly, dogs give humans the purest form of love.

That purest form of love may have started somewhere around 40,000 years ago. There are many theories about the precise moment when dogs became domesticated. But it was long before Steve Jobs developed the iPhone and well after fire was discovered.

Most theorists agree that dogs descended from wolves, with some anthropologists referring to this as the "Big Bark Theory." They believe wolves sought out carcasses left behind by human hunters, leading wolves to hang around humans simply out of necessity and survival. Surprisingly, wolves began playing a role in the hunt, and thankfully, dogs were domesticated somewhere along the way. I wonder which Neanderthal threw the first stick or initiated belly rubs.

It doesn't matter how dogs evolved into the fun-loving, stick-chasing, couch-slobbering, sandwich-stealing animals of today. They arrived, and we love them to pieces. They have fulfilled a role in our society like no other creature on this planet, and we owe them a huge debt of gratitude, which I feel will never be repaid.

Dogs fearlessly jump out of helicopters to save people, sniff out bombs or narcotics in airports, assist police in apprehending criminals, travel with the military to war-torn countries, sniff out illegal drugs, assist the disabled, and most recently, we have trained dogs to detect Covid. How can we possibly repay dogs? It's simple: we can start by not hurting them, and by lending them a helping hand when they become homeless.

I believe people are inherently good. This may be why there are so many people involved in animal advocacy. People who want to stop a dog's suffering and enrich its life. I believe helping a homeless dog also helps people feel good. And we all need to feel good from time to time.

WISHFUL THINKING

At the top of my wish list would be for every rescue dog to have a loving home. But the reality is, this will never happen. Rescue organizations and shelters will always have homeless dogs, and as you have read in this book, it's a complicated journey to becoming homeless. But all is not lost; there are many things we can do to help enrich the lives of all dogs. And some of those things may help slow the increase in homeless dogs in North America.

There should be stricter penalties for animal abusers, such as a lifetime ban from owning animals, automatic jail sentences, substantial fines (donated to rescue organizations), and an open, published list of names of convicted animal abusers. Some of these abused dogs end up in rescues, with organizations dedicating valuable time and funds to help rehabilitate and rehome the dogs.

There should be a global ban on electrical shock collars, prong collars, and choke chains. And a complete nullification and reversal of all Breed-Specific Bans. Dogs from breed bans and offensive training methods often find themselves in shelters and rescues. Again, the organizations that fight to save them must first attempt to eliminate the effects of adverse and painful training methods inflicted on the dogs. And the traumatized dogs from breed bans must be cared for and lovingly rehomed.

There should be legal guidelines or regulations for rescue organizations and shelters to adhere to. I used to think regulations were unnecessary if people used common sense when rescuing and rehoming dogs. But in the absence of common sense, regulations may be required. Rescue organizations and shelters doing right by the dogs in their care have nothing to worry about. But organizations who put the public at risk, do not take their dogs back, offer very little information about the dog, have no veterinary records, or do not keep dogs in foster care need to be held accountable.

Breeders need to be held accountable for every dog they produce. Breeders must take a legal, lifetime responsibility for every dog they produce. This includes backyard breeders, mass dog farms, dog factories, and kennel club registered breeders.

I would like to see the end of dog shows and the harmful breed requirements such as tail or ear docking that they enforce. Dog shows only cause a rise in breeding by mass dog farmers, BYBs or dog factories, for the dog breed that wins best-in-show. Ethical or preservation breeders do not jump on the bandwagon for the fashionable breed.

Lastly, I have always believed you have two responsibilities in life: legal and moral. I feel breeders should have both responsibilities attached to their establishments.

FINAL WORDS

I hope after reading this book you agree that rescue dogs are not damaged; they have been let down by humans. Every one of these dogs deserves a chance for a happy, fulfilled life with humans who will protect them from harm.

There is no better way to show our appreciation for dogs than by finding a homeless dog a forever-home. Watching a rescue dog flourish and thrive in a loving home is the rewarding side of rescue. That is the sole reason people become involved in animal advocacy—going the distance to save a homeless dog and providing them with a second opportunity, or even a first-time chance to live the best possible life. Dogs have rightfully earned a place in our society.

I can say dogs have enriched my life and even saved my life. I hope to spend the rest of my life defending, rescuing, and advocating on their behalf.

The last three stories are about cherished and comical rescue dogs my husband and I have adopted over the years.

"You don't want to simply save a dog,
you want the dog to thrive."
~Tracy Jessiman~

HARLEY

"The Best Things in Life Are Rescued"
~unknown~

Our first rescue dog was an energetic seven-year-old yellow Labrador retriever named Harley. He was surrendered to a rescue organization because the children had grown and moved out of the home. The parents felt they could no longer provide a home for him. Harley was the perfect addition to our family, and we loved him.

No one forgets their first love, whether it has two legs or four, and Harley was our first love rescue dog. He was a handsome, affectionate, master-shedding machine that showed no interest in pleasing us. Harley had a vast, trouble-loving heart, and he had two monkeys with a banjo in his head instead of a functioning brain. He lived his life with great enthusiasm and never looked back to see the train wreck he left behind. He certainly loved us and everyone he met, but he especially loved our black Labrador retriever named Sam.

Sam and Harley were inseparable. They ate, played, and slept together. But we saw a noticeable difference in their training—or lack of training, in Harley's case. Sam had completed puppy classes and two levels of obedience, which he passed with flying colors. Although Harley was enthusiastically friendly and did not have a bad bone in his body, he lacked boundaries. In the first month with us, we took Harley to our veterinarian twice because we were convinced he was deaf. The vet reassured us Harley was not deaf, just stubborn.

We discovered, quite early, that Harley was a humper. It was a habit we could not correct because we didn't know when it would happen or to who. Harley would try to hump Sam, but Sam would quickly sit down, ruining Harley's fun. He never humped my husband or me, but random pillows, couches, or the cat's post were fair game. He tried to hump our eight-year-old niece, and when I tried to get Harley off her back, she said, "Its ok, Aunt Tracy; I love it when Harley hugs me."

Many rescues and shelters make obedience classes mandatory when adopting out a dog. Not because the dog needs the training but because that time in obedience class can be essential for bonding with the new dog. It also helps the new owner learn how to communicate with the dog. In Harley's case, he did not have mandatory obedience instructions, but we moved forward with the classes out of sheer desperation.

We put both dogs in the same obedience class, hoping Harley would mimic Sam's stellar behavior, but it was an epic failure. Harley barked so much during the first class that he threw up in the gym. The trainer recommended the participants conduct the session outside in the second class because, "It may help that barking dog from last week." It didn't help, and it became the most embarrassing moment of my entire life.

As the class proceeded outdoors, my husband instantly staked his claim for the ever-obedient Sam, leaving me at the mercy of Harley. At the start, the other dog owners, as usual, stood in a circle with their dogs quietly sitting by their sides. Harley couldn't sit as he was too interested in the kid's baseball game on the other side of the field, but he wasn't barking. As the trainer started the class, a kid hit a baseball over our group. Harley took off in hot pursuit of the ball, dragging me through the circle of dog owners.

When I got to my feet, I was mortified to find my t-shirt around my neck tangled in my bra, with my breasts on full display. I finished the six weeks of obedience lessons out of sheer spite, with our marriage intact, my breasts kept under wraps, and our unshakeable commitment to "that barking dog" remaining. Even though Harley passed his obedience classes, he was never the perfect dog and life with him was full of endless negotiations.

Harley loved children and was incredibly gentle around them. We often thought he must have truly loved those years with his previous owners when their children were young. Our nieces and nephews could dress Harley up in anything they found, and Harley would sit patiently, relishing all the attention.

Harley was a unique and quirky pet, so of course he did the unthinkable: he bolted out our front door. Our neighbor was coming out of her home simultaneously, so Harley ran into her house. He ran up their stairs, through every room of their lovely (pet-free) home, including jumping across their bed. He then ran back out their front door (with my neighbor, in shock, still holding her door open) and ran back into our home. Our neighbor thanked me for the entertainment by never speaking to me again.

Sometimes a rescue dog will bond more closely with one person. In our case, Harley always wanted more attention and affection from my husband. God forbid if I tried to hug my husband because Harley would lose his mind trying to get between us. Because of this, we always locked our bedroom door before sex, considering that Harley might try to kill me.

My husband always thought I favored Sam, but I truly loved both dogs. Life with Sam was just easier. I could take Sam to the park and throw a ball all day, and he'd always return to me. One day my husband showed up at the park with Harley. He thought Harley would love to run with Sam and chase the ball. I warned my husband not to drop the leash, but he didn't listen. He threw the ball, and Harley ran past it and kept on running. We had to get the car to chase him down and capture him. It felt so good to say, "I told you so." But the joke was on me. That night, I let Harley out for a midnight pee and he made his escape. My husband had left the gate open, and Harley took the opportunity and ran down the street, with me in hot pursuit. When I caught up with him, I ripped the belt off my housecoat and used it as a leash to get Harley home. The following morning, my neighbor called me to tell me she and her husband cracked up when they saw me half-naked running through the neighborhood after my blond monster.

One of Harley's favorite pastimes was going on our boat with my husband as if they were on a date. My husband, for many years, would take Harley to a secluded beach that kept Harley safe from running away and they could safely play fetch on the ocean. On one occasion, Harley swam back to shore, dropped the ball, and ran past my husband. As my husband turned around, he saw what was about to happen and knew it would be devastating for someone. Harley was running towards a bride and her wedding party who had just set up for ocean-side wedding pictures. The bride saw the sopping wet, dirty, sand-covered, barking Harley running towards her. She hiked up her beautiful dress and ran down the beach with her bridesmaids, groomsmen, and new husband running along behind her. Luckily, my husband snatched Harley just before he ruined a beautiful wedding dress. I often wonder if the couple shares that story with people or even their children by now.

One memorable vacation with Harley tuned into a hilarious tale. We had recently installed a brand-new metal pet barrier to ensure Harley and Sam were safe in the vehicle. We packed our SUV with wine, beer, a cooler of food, luggage, and everything we needed for the cottage. The last items to pack were the dogs and they eagerly jumped in the vehicle.

Harley was a bit of a barker in any vehicle, but Sam could usually settle him down by leaning into him and resting his head on Harley's back. This act alone seemed to calm and comfort Harley. But for some unknown reason, on this trip Harley decided to shove his way through the pet barrier and jumped over the back seat onto my husband's lap while he was driving on a four-lane highway. My husband didn't say a word as I grabbed Harley's collar to stop him from licking Earl's face and putting us in the ditch. And while this was happening, I could see Sam sitting in the back at the back of the SUV staring at Harley in complete disbelief.

We had to pull over (when it was safe), repack the whole truck and start on our four-hour drive again. This was the only time Harley didn't bark in the vehicle. I would have paid good money to get inside Harley's head to understand how he operated. His crazy shenanigans always happened sporadically and without warning.

Harley made every Christmas special, but one, in particular, he made memorable for the whole family. Luckily, our family remembers it with great humor. We were hosting our entire family of ten for Christmas Eve dinner. The next day, Christmas dinner would be at my mother-in-law's, with traditional turkey and ham, so I decided to make a double-sized homemade lasagna that festive evening.

With the table set, Caesar salad, lasagna, rolls, and apple pie made and set aside, I took my shower before the family was set to arrive and got dressed. I opened some wine and checked on the food. Harley was sitting on the couch looking out the window, and shockingly, he was not barking at anyone on the street. On reflection, I should have known something was desperately wrong.

I checked on my oversized lasagna, which I had left on top of the stove to cool, only to find when I lifted the tinfoil, the lasagna was gone. Harley had eaten every last bite without spilling anything on the counter or floor. I still don't know how he got his fat head under the hot tinfoil, but he did. Mission accomplished.

I didn't say a word to Harley because what did it matter? The lasagna was missing in action, and getting mad wouldn't achieve anything. I went to the living room, and all Harley did was roll over on his back, wag his tail, and rub the remnants of tomato sauce from his face into my new beige couch. Our family ate hot dogs that Christmas Eve.

Harley lived the rest of his life with us, and his antics live in our hearts forever—from eating a dead snake (I spent the better part of a week gagging every time I looked at him) to barking at the pizza guy so much that he threatened to stop delivering to our home. We also had to replace the screen on our sliding back door more than five times one summer because Harley kept running through it every time a leaf, squirrel, or bird (real or imaginary) moved. He also slept under our bed for many years, affectionately labelled Harley's bunk bed.

We treasure every memory of Harley, and we talk fondly about him. Even though he has been gone for many years, and we have had other dogs, Harley was our first rescue dog. We genuinely believe we gave him a loving home, and he showed us how thankful he was by loving us unconditionally and never acknowledging his name. He was the very best bad dog.

PORSCHE

*"Love is not a matter of counting the years,
but making the years count."*
~unknown~

My husband and I adopted Porsche, who had spent seven years living in a barn and manufacturing puppies for a dog farmer. After an emergency caesarian, she was discarded like garbage when she could no longer produce income. He threw a Free-To-Good home ad in the local community paper. A woman responded, and the owner said, "She's in crate number eight in the barn. Pick her up before I get home." The woman did just that, but once she got home, she realized that she was ill-prepared to own a dog, as she had two small children. She contacted a rescue organization, and they raced to collect the dog.

Porsche was fostered by a dear friend who shared all of Porsche's journey with me; the poor girl's nails were so long she had trouble navigating on floors, she was uncertain of indoor life, and she wasn't house trained due to living in a barn. My friend helped Porsche gain some confidence and learn how to be a member of a loving family, and in less than twenty-four hours, her adoptive dogs had Porsche house-trained.

We adopted Porsche, and my friend visited her many times. Her husband still carries a picture of Porsche in his wallet. Porsche was a sweet girl who wanted nothing more than to lay her head on your lap. She loved her stuffed toys and would carry one with her when we went for walks. One day, she dropped one of her toys in a can of paint while we were painting the handrail in our home. She was devastated, and I could not get mad at her when I saw the look on her sweet face, even with the paint splashed on my walls. She learned she didn't have to be afraid of the noises made by my blow dryer, vacuum cleaner, or microwave. We often referred to Porsche as the mime-dog, as she never barked.

She excelled as a Therapy Dog and was always the favorite when on an official visit. People could not help but be drawn to her as she was a beautiful dog who would lie on her back, often falling asleep, during her retirement home visits. Blonds really do have more fun.

Porsche gave as much of herself as possible and asked for nothing in return. This girl wanted to please everyone she met, and she accomplished that every day. I took her to my office many times, where she wandered from office to office, greeting everyone she met. She also quickly figured out which office had treats. The women I worked with could not believe how cuddly, calm, and quiet this girl was.

You could bathe Porsche, clip her nails, brush her fur, and even take her to the vet. Nothing bothered this girl. She went on many holidays with us, swimming in the ocean or a private pool. She didn't discriminate as long as water was involved. She loved other dogs and would entice them to play with her by showing off her zoomies. She shared her toys, beds, and personal space with any dog, but she never allowed other dogs to sniff her butt. It was the only time she would bark, just one loud bark telling them to stop. It was the only hang-up she had from being a breeding girl for all those years. Aside from that, she tolerated everything except her meals being late.

As a former breeding dog, we always thought Porsche was not allowed to bark. This is often the case at extensive breeding facilities where they yell at the dogs or hit them to make them stop barking. Porsche was hilarious when we were out for walks and another dog would get in her face and bark. Porsche, many times, would turn around and sit on the dog to make it stop barking.

Porsche was a bit of a Velcro dog and had to be wherever I happened to be, which also meant she wouldn't chase a ball. She would bring a ball to me, wait for me to throw it and watch it go through the air, but she'd turn her attention back to us. We always felt that, if a bubble were to appear above her head, it would have said, "Why would I run away when you're right here?" Then she would sit or lie down on both my feet.

We were blessed to have her as our companion for many years, and we still believe she was just too good to be true. She would have lived forever if tears and love could have saved her.

SHEENA

"I love dogs with missing parts!"
~Claire Ford, age 7~

This blind beauty drifted into our lives when I was assigned, by a rescue organization, to be her dedicated driver because her foster mom did not have a car. I happily took Sheena to all her medical appointments and dropped off food, medicine, or supplies as needed. I enjoyed every visit with Sheena and found myself hoping that I would need to make that drive each morning. Sheena and I quickly developed a remarkable and deep bond, which continues to flourish today.

Sheena came from one of the best and most responsible local rescue organizations. Not many organizations are equipped to care for a blind dog or are willing to take on the responsibility. But they happily took Sheena under their wing and into their care.

Over the following weeks, the rescue organization decided to move Sheena to my home to continue her foster care. We had a particularly nasty winter that year and the rescue thought it might be easier on Sheena as I also worked from home most days. My husband and I talked beforehand about bringing a blind dog into our home. He has seen legions of foster dogs through our house, but he was hesitant with Sheena. He was worried that he would be too emotional looking at a blind dog every day, but he agreed to foster her. We also had a friendly yellow lab who had met Sheena, and they got along marvellously, so Sheena moved in as a foster dog.

Having Sheena as a foster dog did not last long—I heard my husband on the phone twenty-four hours later telling his friends he couldn't believe how sweet this dog was and that he found her to be so inspirational. After that call, I knew Sheena had found her forever home. We agreed to adopt her and happily became foster-fails.

Having a rescue dog like Sheena affected our whole family, but especially our teenaged nephew, Evan. Sheena came to live with us while Evan was in the hospital having invasive, lifesaving surgery. When my husband and I were called to say we could visit Evan, we jumped in the car and sped to the hospital. We entered Evan's room and saw his parents and friends standing around his bed holding balloons. The first words out of Evan's mouth were – "How is Sheena? I can't wait to meet her!" My husband just about crumbled so I updated Evan on Sheena.

Initially, our veterinarian was unsure if Sheena was blind or, because she had been starved, her eyes had sunken into her eye sockets. A three-hour drive to an animal ophthalmologist confirmed the devastating news: her eyeballs were gone. Our veterinary clinic performed an Enucleation surgery where they cleaned the sockets and permanently stitched the eyes closed. It's a routine surgery for dogs who suffer from glaucoma, those diagnosed with eye cancer, or because of eye trauma. In Sheena's case, it was brutal trauma. She recovered from the surgery and was much more comfortable afterwards as she had been scratching at her eyes, but that stopped.

Sheena came from deplorable conditions. To claim that she went from a junkyard to a life at Shangri-La is a gross misrepresentation; a junkyard would have been a safer environment for her than where she grew up.

Sheena lived her life tied to a dilapidated trailer and her unprecedented rescue was complicated by the horrifically dangerous environment she lived in. This poor girl had been neglected, starved, blinded, over-bred, and forced to fend for herself outside at the end of a chain. I will never understand how people can do such horrendous things to a defenseless creature. Yet, even with everything she was forced to live through, she still loves everyone she meets, especially children.

People who meet Sheena cannot believe she had such a terrible existence before we adopted her, as her disposition is one of the sweetest anyone has ever encountered. She is now a registered Therapy Dog who loves visiting retirement homes, and universities during exam time. She is also a registered member of the blood donor program. The program collects blood that is used for emergencies and surgeries. Sheena donated multiple times over the years, but one donation, in particular, stands out.

I received a call one Friday afternoon from the animal emergency hospital. They had a dog in need of a live dog-to-dog blood transfusion. Sheena answered the bell, and my best friend saved someone else's best friend. The owners of the dog Sheena saved contacted me through the clinic. They bought Sheena a lovely gift, and we are all friends to this day.

A local television station heard about Sheena, and they filmed her for the evening news. The broadcast showcased her loving personality as two neighborhood children walked her around the block and played with her.

She plays with toys just like any other dog by throwing them around. She then tilts her head to hear where they land and pounces on them. She loves long walks, rolling on her back, belly rubs, car rides, and she is obsessed with my husband. She snores when she's sleeping, makes Jurassic Park sounds when playing with her toys, and never wants to miss out on an adventure. She's happiest when our home is full of people, yet she's the best girl when home alone. She's a super happy girl, and she has become the poster child of success for rescue organizations and disabled dogs. She's simply the best, and we cannot imagine a world without her. I could say, when it comes to Sheena, we have love in the third degree.

"What feels like the end, is often just the beginning."
~unknown~

ACKNOWLEDGMENTS

This book would not have been possible without the support and encouragement of my favorite husband, Earl. Our marriage survived my two-year writing extravaganza. When I finished the book, his skillful editing began. I remember handing him my book and losing my mind as he crossed out words and whole paragraphs. Earl, in the end, your editing was precise and exactly what the book needed. Thank you, I love you, please take the dog for a walk.

Of course, thank you to the families and individuals who shared their tender rescue dog stories with me. This book would not have been possible without your participation and trust. Thank you.

I owe a debt of gratitude to the Halifax Chronicle Herald and the Saltwire Network. I appreciate your unwavering support to advocate for animal rescue in your paper and on your media platforms.

A special thank you to the gregarious Todd Veinotte for his endless support. Todd generously opened his airwaves for me, from his radio talk show on City News 95.7 to his branded Podcast innumerable times. In typical Todd fashion, he openly and honestly provides both sides to all topics. Without Todd's support, many animal rescue stories would never have been shared with the public. I remain forever thankful.

I also want to thank Russell Mackenzie and Frankie Hollywood. Both radio personalities welcomed me daily, for many years, to highlight homeless pets on their airwaves. I appreciate your support, but especially the side-splitting laughter.

Thank you to my friend Elizabeth Andrews. She took the time to proofread my manuscript and offered valuable input to this book. She did all of this while working, tending to her three rescue dogs and her never-ending rotation of foster dogs. Liz, you are a blessing. She is also responsible for the photo featured on the cover of this book. Her beloved rescue dog named Tuk.

Thank you to the many rescuers, volunteers, advocates, fosters, shelter staff, veterinarians, adopters, veterinary staff, and individuals who operate rescue organizations who openly shared their stories with me. This book is for you.

Finally, to the rescue dog that changed the trajectory of my heart, Sheena, my blind beauty. You arrived in rescue starved, blinded, broken, over-bred, and released from a chained, lonely existence. You blossomed with our love and support. You became a Therapy Dog and a cherished comical member of our family. You were the inspiration for me to write this book. You also made my abusive past disappear when I witnessed how you forgave humans for what they did to you. I am and will remain eternally grateful because, in the end, you saved me.

RESCUE FAMILIES

*"Be the reason someone believes
in the goodness of people."*
~unknown~

The best life-altering thing to ever happen to a rescue dog is finding a loving forever home. A home where they are no longer cold, nervous, lonely, or unloved. A home where they can thrive and grow old, which is what happened for every rescue dog in this book. The true champions and unsung heroes of rescue are the people who adopt homeless dogs.

Here are the unsung rescue heroes:

Angel	Cheryl & Logan White
Badger	Shawn & Michelle Cleary
Brooklyn	Stacy & Joey Chisholm
Calvin	Carol & Tim Houston
Charlie	Elizabeth Andrews
Chelsea	The Sutton Family
Chewie	Julian, Emma, Jessica, Jack & Charlotte Warr (photo Jody O'Brien)
Crystal	Karen & Doug Balser
Daisy	Jamie J. Ollivier & Danielle Blackwood
Dyson	Stacey & Joey Chisholm
Eddie	Arron, Heidi & Liam Butler
Harley	Tracy & Earl Jessiman
Henry	Joan Warren & Sid Richdale
Jaxson	Sean & Michelle Kelly

Jeb	Bonnie Ashton & Michael Kearney
Little	Jo-Anne & Brent Landsburg
Lollie	Stacey & Joey Chisholm
Max	Stephanie, Matt, Jack & Beth Hall
Mojo	Leta & Joey Wagner
Mumford	Tammy & Stephen Nauss
Nash	Carol & Tim Houston
Newman	Joan Warren & Sid Richdale
Otis	Joan Warren & Sid Richdale
Pipsqueak	Ashley & Shane McWhirter
Porsche	Tracy & Earl Jessiman
Raider	Elizabeth Andrews
Redgy	Kelly, Peter, Madeline & Juliet Nolet
Rosie	Scott Baker & Beth Blakeney-Baker
Rucker	Cheryl Hamilton & Dion Kelderman *(Larissa & Hayden)*
Sadie	Ashely & Shane McWhirter
Sheena	Tracy & Earl Jessiman
Silver	Gareth Meagher
Toby	Frankie Hollywood
Tuk	Elizabeth Andrews
Tucker	Kate, Kevin & Mary Ward
Wally	Elizabeth Andrews
Winnie	Frankie Hollywood
Winnie	Carol & Tim Houston

TIPS FOR FINDING A RESPONSIBLE RESCUE

- the organization responds to all questions and inquiries
- the rescue volunteers are happy, with positive attitudes
- there is an established Board of Directors
- the organization has a good reputation
- there is an active fundraising strategy
- the rescue has a proven palliative care program
- the organization has a "No Kill" designation
- the rescue supports a lifetime commitment for every dog
- every dog has been in an approved foster home
- all dogs receive health checks by approved veterinarians
- all dogs are spayed or neutered (this is the responsibility of the rescue for puppies)
- health and medical records are offered to the adopter
- the rescue is familiar with the individual dog's temperament
- there is a rigorous screening process of all potential adopters (reference, home visit, etc.)
- the organization is registered as a not-for-profit or charitable operation
- the rescue is patient and thorough during the evaluation process, it isn't a race
- be sure to read the application carefully, as it will hold a wealth of information about the organization

TIPS FOR FINDING A RESPONSIBLE BREEDER

- meet the breeder and the breeding dogs, and tour the facility
- the facility should be clean
- the breeder should be willing to answer all your questions
- the breeder is a valuable source of knowledge, information, and education
- the breeder should provide a list of what to expect as the puppy develops
- they should have extensive knowledge of the breed
- they should breed only one specific breed
- health guarantees should be offered for every dog
- the breeder should provide veterinary references
- all breeding dogs should be at least two years old
- only one litter bred at a time
- there should be extensive health screening and testing at the facility
- the breeder can provide medical history, genealogy, and lineage records for the breeding dogs
- the dogs are not bred multiple times in a calendar year
- the puppies and breeding dogs live indoors as if they are pets
- the puppies do not leave until two months old
- the breeder sells their dogs directly to the buyer, no middleman
- the breeder will take back the dog if you can no longer care for it and will subsequently rehome the dog

ACRONYMS & DEFINITIONS

Adoption – A wonderful alternative to buying from a breeder.
Adoption Application – The most rewarding paperwork you will ever complete.
Adoption Fee – Best money you will ever spend.
Advocate – Someone who never sleeps.
Altered dog – A spayed or neutered dog.
Animal Control – Help for lost dogs or dogs taken in from cruelty seizures.
Bait Dog – Used to train fighting dogs.
Boomerang Dog – Dog that is returned to rescue.
Breeder – A profit-focused business.
BSL – Breed Specific Legislation.
BYB – Back Yard Breeder.
Choke Chain – Harmful metal chain link collar that chokes the dog when they pull.
Compassion Fatigue – Emotionally exhausted.
DNA - Do Not Adopt (specific individuals such as known animal abusers).
Dog – The most amazing animal on the planet.
Dog Farm – Also known as puppy mill, mass dog farming, or dog factory.
Donations – The lifeblood for saving homeless pets.
E-Collar – Sends painful shocks or buzzing to a dog's neck.
Electric Fence – An invisible fence that works with an e-collar.
Foster – A temporary home for a dog before adoption.
Foster Failure – When a foster family cannot possibly part with their fostered dog.
Fundraising – Essential for every rescue and shelter's survival.

Fur – Doggy glitter.
Gotcha Day – Better than birthdays. Anniversary for the day your dog was adopted.
High-kill Shelter – Self-explanatory.
Home Visit – Quick home inspection of the home of a potential adopter.
Husband – I love him, and he helps walk the dog.
Kennel Clubs – Registry service exclusively for purebred dogs.
Keyboard Warrior – Does nothing for rescue, same effectiveness as screaming in traffic.
Meat Dog – Dogs raised or stolen for human consumption.
No-Kill Shelter – Euthanize only for illness or public safety.
Owner Surrender – Dogs surrendered from homes.
Pandemic Puppy – Puppies acquired during the Covid pandemic.
Paw – A valuable tool for counter surfing.
Prong Collar – Metal collar with prongs that inflict pain on a dog's neck.
Preservation Breeder – produce quality, healthy dogs.
Purebred – Dogs bred with the same breed, and have proven documented genealogy.
Rescue – A private organization that supports re-homing dogs.
Rescue Dog – A lovingly re-homed dog.
Service Dog – Highly trained dog that works with the police or disabled people, etc.
Shelter – A brick-and-mortar building that houses rescue dogs.
Special Needs – A dog that may be blind, deaf, has three legs, may have wheels, one eye, or requires a specialized diet.
Stray – Homeless/lost dog.
Street Dog – Homeless and may be feral.
Tail – Used to clear coffee tables.
Temperament Testing – Qualified trainer assesses the demeanor or attitude of a dog.
Therapy Dog – A dog that has been tested and certified for organized visits to retirement homes, universities, etc.
Vet Check – New-to-rescue dogs are taken to a veterinarian for a health exam.
Veterinary Clinic – A place where some dogs turn into Tasmanian Devils.
Volunteer – The closest thing to an angel on earth.

SOURCES

"If animals spoke, humanity would cry."
~Manuj Rajput~

Chapter 1 – Making a Rescuer

Leggate, J. (2020, October 7). "Escaped dog briefly shuts down runway at Toronto airport." Fox News. Retrieved from: https://www.foxnews.com/travel/escaped-dog-flights-toronto-airport

Coffey, H. (2020, October 8). "Escaped dog caused 'chaos' at Toronto Airport, Grounding All Flights for An Hour." Independent. Retrieved from: https://www.independent.co.uk/travel/news-and-advice/toronto-airport-dog-escape-crystal-canada-b880810.html

Mulligan, P. (2020, October 6). "Boy, could she run! Pearson airport leads effort to find Spanish podenco." Canadian Broadcasting Corporation. Retrieved from: https://www.cbc.ca/news/canada/nova-scotia/pearson-airport-leads-effort-find-crystal-spanish-podenco-1.5751189

Chapter 2 – Creating a Rescue Dog

Brandt, K. (n.d.). "Why Are Dogs Given Up." Pet Finder. Retrieved from: https://www.petfinder.com/pet-adoption/dog-adoption/pets-relinquished-shelters/

Miller, P. (2012, July 10). "Dog Rehoming: When Is It The Right Decision?" Whole Dog Journal. Retrieved from:

https://www.whole-dog-journal.com/lifestyle/dog-rehoming-when-is-it-the-right-decision/

Naqi, K. (2008, November 21). "Vick in Virginia to face state charges; deal would yield no jail time." ESPN and The Associated Press. Retrieved from: https://www.espn.com/nfl/news/story?id=3717312

Giambalvo, E. (2019, September 18). "How Michael Vicks dogfighting case changed animal welfare." Washington Post. Retrieved from: https://www.washingtonpost.com/graphics/2019/sports/michael-vick-dogfighting-dogs/

Best Friends Animal Society. (n.d.). "The brave, beautiful dogs rescued from Michael Vick's Bad Newz Kennel." Retrieved from: https://bestfriends.org/sanctuary/about-sanctuary/vicktory-dogs

Matas, R. & Dhillon, S. (2011, January 31). "Post-Olympic slaughter of 70 sled dogs prompts rage, embarrassment." *The Globe and Mail*. Retrieved from: https://www.theglobeandmail.com/news/british-columbia/post-olympic-slaughter-of-70-sled-dogs-prompts-rage-embarrassment/article564379/

Canadian Broadcast Corporation. (2012, November 21). "BC Sled Dog Slaughter Sentence Appalls SPCA." Retrieved from: https://www.cbc.ca/news/canada/british-columbia/b-c-sled-dog-slaughter-sentence-appalls-spca-1.127765

Fern Levitt (Director). Documentary: *Sled Dogs*. CCI Entertainment. (2016, December 3).

Verongos, H. (2017, July 27). "*Sled Dogs* Exposes Abuse of Working Animals." *The New York Times*. Retrieved from: https://www.nytimes.com/2017/07/27/movies/sled-dogs-review.html

Humane Society International. (n.d.). "Stop the Suffering: End the Slaughter." Retrieved from: https://www.hsi.org/issues/dog-meat-trade/

SOI Dog. (n.d.). "Stop the Torture and Slaughter of Man's Best Friend." Retrieved from: https://www.soidog.org/content/end-dog-meat-trade

British Broadcasting Corporation. (2017, April 17). "The countries where people still eat cats and dogs for dinner." Retrieved from: https://www.bbc.com/news/newsbeat-39577557

Petras, G. (2019, February 25). "South Koreans eat more than 1 million dogs each year – but that's slowly changing. Here's why." *USA Today*. Retrieved from: https://www.usatoday.com/in-depth/news/2019/02/25/south-koreans-eat-more-than-2-million-dogs-every-year-but-thats-changing/2930025002/

Yam, K. (2019, December 17). "Asian Americans call on NBC to cut ties with Jay Leno after dog-eating joke." National Broadcast Corporation. Retrieved from: https://www.nbcnews.com/news/asian-america/asian-americans-call-nbc-cut-ties-jay-leno-after-dog-n1103516

Hannon, B. P. D. (2021, March 24). "Jay Leno apologizes to Asians for decades of jokes that promoted stereotypes and were made as recently as 2020." *Daily Mail*. Retrieved from:

https://www.dailymail.co.uk/news/article-9399003/Jay-Leno-apologizes-Asian-Americans-decades-jokes-community.html

Hattam, J. (2021, March 18). "'They see them as fellow citizens': How Istanbul's street dogs have found a place in society." *Washington Post*. Retrieved from:

https://www.washingtonpost.com/travel/2021/03/18/istanbul-turkey-dogs-stray-documentary/

Hobart, E. (2021, November 5). "Morocco has 3 million stray dogs. Meet the people trying to help them." *National Geographic*. Retrieved from:

https://www.nationalgeographic.com/animals/article/meet-the-people-helping-morocco-stray-dogs

Golden Rescue. (n.d.). "Istanbul: A Rescue Mission of Love." https://www.goldenrescue.ca/2015/12/istanbul-a-rescue-mission-of-love/

Mowatt, T. (2018, February). "Saving Spanish Greyhounds. Rescue groups offer hope for used and abused 'disposable dogs'." The Bark. Retrieved from: https://thebark.com/content/saving-spanish-greyhounds

Johns, T. (2022, March 26). "Bay Area non-profit helps save hundreds of animals stuck in war-torn Ukraine." ABC 7 News. Retrieved from: https://abc7news.com/ukraine-dogs-stranded-nonprofit-saving-animals-how-to-help/11682041/

Canadian Broadcasting Corporation. (2022, February 1). "Planeload of abandoned dogs and cats from Afghanistan arrives in Vancouver." Retrieved from: https://www.cbc.ca/news/canada/british-columbia/bc-afghanistan-animal-arrival-1.6336121

Schweig, S. C. (2017, October 19). "Huskies rescued from war-torn city get their very first beds. They were found wandering in streets in Syria." The Dodo. Retrieved from: https://www.thedodo.com/close-to-home/huskies-aleppo-zoo-rescue-toronto

Webb, B. (2021, May 3). "HALO Animal Rescue group helps find forever homes in the U.S. for stray dogs in Mexico." Fox10 Phoenix. Retrieved from: https://www.fox10phoenix.com/news/halo-animal-rescue-group-helps-find-forever-homes-in-the-u-s-for-stray-dogs-in-mexico

Lee, F. (2014, February 23). "Stray puppies from India find shelter in Minn." *USA Today*. Retrieved from: https://www.usatoday.com/story/news/nation/2014/02/23/stray-puppies-from-india-find-shelter-in-minn/5730769/

Fred Levy (photographer). (2015). "The Black Dogs Project." Race Point.

Pet Finder. (n.d.). "Black Dog Syndrome." Retrieved from: https://www.petfinder.com/pet-adoption/dog-adoption/black-dog-syndrome/#:~:text=BDS%20is%20observed%20by%20shelters,the%20shelter%20and%20rescue%20population.

Mullins, N. (n.d.). "What to do About Compassion Fatigue." Pet Finder. Retrieved from: https://www.petfinder.com/pro/for-shelters/compassion-fatigue/

Bekoff, M. PhD. (2019, April 25)."Should Dogs Be Shocked, Choked, or Pronged?" Psychology Today. Retrieved from: https://www.psychologytoday.com/ca/blog/animal-emotions/201904/should-dogs-be-shocked-choked-or-pronged

Madson. C. (2019, January 29 – Updated 2022, March 8). "Dog Training Aversives: What Are They and Why Should You Avoid Them?" Preventive Vet. Retrieved from: https://www.preventivevet.com/dogs/dog-training-aversives

Dickson, Courtney. (2019, February 22) "B.C. SPCA calls on pet owners to toss shock collars." Canadian Broadcast Corporation. Retrieved from: https://www.cbc.ca/news/canada/british-columbia/spca-shock-collar-1.5029174

Frank. (2022, March 22) "What Countries Have Banned Shock Collars?" The Dog Central. Retrieved from: https://thedogcentral.com/what-countries-have-banned-shock-collars/

Todd, Zazie PhD. (2018, June 20) "Study outlines reason to ban electric collars for dogs." Companion Animal Psychology. Retrieved from: https://www.companionanimalpsychology.com/2018/06/study-outlines-reasons-to-ban.html

Block, K. & Amundson, S. (2022, July 18). "Breaking: Historic transport of approximately 4,000 beagles spared from animal testing." A Human World. Retrieved from: https://blog.humanesociety.org/2022/07/breaking-historic-transport-of-approximately-4000-beagles-spared-from-animal-testing.html?credit=blog_post_071822_id12963

Price, J. T. (2022, July 21). "4,000 Beagles Were Rescued from a Virginia Research Facility. How Common Is Lab Testing on Dogs in the U.S.?" News@Northeastern. Retrieved from: https://news.northeastern.edu/2022/07/21/beagles-lab-testing/

Animal Humane Society (n.d.) "Animal hoarding: What it is, what it isn't, and how you can help." Animal Humane Society. Retrieved from: https://www.animalhumanesociety.org/news/animal-hoarding-what-it-what-it-isnt-and-how-you-can-help

Frost, Randy PhD. (2000, April1) "People Who Hoard Animals." Psychiatric Times. Retrieved from: https://www.psychiatrictimes.com/view/people-who-hoard-animals

Pearlmen, Mischa (2018, July 20) "This Heartbreaking Tale Shows Why You Shouldn't Offer Up Pets As 'Free To A Good Home'." Lad Bible. Retrieved from: https://www.ladbible.com/news/animals-a-tale-shows-why-you-shouldnt-offer-up-pets-free-to-a-good-home-20180720

Gray, Allison (2015, June 30) "Enough Is Enough: Why 'Free to a Good Home' Ads Must Die." Petful. Retrieved from: https://www.petful.com/animal-welfare/free-to-a-good-home/

Chapter 3 – The Ugly Side of Dog Breeding

Humane Society. (n.d.). "Stopping Puppy Mills." Retrieved from: https://www.humanesociety.org/all-our-fights/stopping-puppy-mills

Best Friends Animal Society. (2018, December 4). "Puppy Mill Rescue Dogs: Transition to Home Life." Retrieved from: https://resources.bestfriends.org/article/puppy-mill-dogs-where-mill-pets-are-sold

Solotaroff, P. (2017, Jan. 3). "The Dog Factory: Inside the Sickening World of Puppy Mills." *Rolling Stone Magazine.* Retrieved from: https://www.rollingstone.com/culture/culture-features/the-dog-factory-inside-the-sickening-world-of-puppy-mills-112161/

Burgos, S. (2021, Nov. 22). "What Is a Puppy Mill? The reality of Pet Shops and Fake Breeders." Daily Paws. Retrieved from: https://www.dailypaws.com/dogs-puppies/dog-adoption/what-is-a-puppy-mill

The Animal Rescue Site. (n.d.). "This Is Why We Fight So Hard Against Backyard Breeding and Puppy Mills." Retrieved from: https://blog.theanimalrescuesite.greatergood.com/backyardbreeding/

Best Friends Sanctuary. (n.d.). "What Is a Puppy Mill?" Retrieved from: https://bestfriends.org/advocacy/ending-puppy-mills/what-puppy-mill

Neff, Michelle. (n.d.) "5 Common Illnesses That Occur in Puppy Mill Dogs and Why You Should ALWAYS Adopt." One Green Planet. Retrieved from: https://www.onegreenplanet.org/animalsandnature/common-illnesses-in-puppy-mill-dogs/

Humane Society Veterinary Medical Association. (n.d.). "Husbandry and Medical Concerns in Puppy Mills." https://www.hsvma.org/husbandry_medical_concerns_puppy_mills%23.VkTfTnarTIU

"This information is adapted from Dr. Lisa Hindle Deppe's presentation "A Veterinarian's Experience with Iowa's Puppy Mill Dogs," as given to the Care of Animals in Commercial Enterprises Legislative Study Committee on September 29, 2009 in support of the proposed Puppy Mill Bill, which recently became law in Iowa."

Farricelli, A. (2021, March 31). "Understanding the Nature versus Nurture Concept in Dogs." Pet Helpful. Retrieved from: https://pethelpful.com/dogs/Understanding-the-Nature-Versus-Nurture-Concept-in-Dogs

Beuchat, C. PhD. (2016, January 17). "Is it Nurture or Nature?" Institute of Canine Biology. Retrieved from: https://www.instituteofcaninebiology.org/blog/is-it-nuture-or-nature

Hekman, J. (2014, October 20). "How a Mother's Stress Can Influence Unborn Puppies." The Whole Dog Journal. Retrieved from: https://www.whole-dog-journal.com/puppies/puppy-health/how-a-mothers-stress-can-influence-unborn-puppies/

Star of Texas Veterinary Hospital. (2021, April 14). "Dog Behavior: How the Past Shapes the Present." Retrieved from: https://staroftexasvet.com/dog-behavior-how-the-past-shapes-the-present/

Humane Decisions. (n.d.). "Puppy Mills, Commercial and Backyard Dog Breeders." Retrieved from: https://www.humanedecisions.com/puppy-mills-commercial-and-backyard-dog-breeders/

Johnson, Mike (2021, September 27). "What Does it Mean to be a Guardian for a Dog?" Pet Play. Retrieved from: https://www.petplay.com/blogs/tips/what-does-it-mean-to-be-a-guardian-for-a-dog

Kane, Laura (2016, Deceber 1). "B.C. Family warns against 'guardian home' after therapy dog taken by breeder. The Globe and Mail. Retrieved from: https://www.theglobeandmail.com/news/british-columbia/bc-family-warns-

against-guardian-homes-after-therapy-dog-taken-by-breeder/
article33131589/

Underwood, Colleen (2020, December 4). "Calgary first responder and dog breeder battle over 18-month-old Australian labradoodle service dog." Canadian Broadcast Network. Retrieved from: https://www.cbc.ca/news/canada/calgary/first-responder-aussiedoodle-breeder-1.5828049

Portia. (2022, August 30). "Pros And Cons Of Being A Guardian Dog Owner." Petovly. Retrieved from: https://petovly.com/pros-and-cons-of-being-a-guardian-dog-owner/

Wright, G. (2015, August 2). "Mennonite puppy mill, Southwestern Ontario, Canada." You Tube. Retrieved from: https://www.youtube.com/watch?v=k5qmEpQzvK8

The Puppy Mill Project. (n.d.). "Amish Puppy Mills." The Puppy Mill Project. Retrieved from: https://www.thepuppymillproject.org/amish-puppy-mills/

NBC News. (2010, January 11). "Activists go undercover to thwart puppy mills." NBC News. Retrieved from: https://www.nbcnews.com/health/health-news/activists-go-undercover-thwart-puppy-mills-flna1c9441313."

Van de Kamp Nohl, M. (2009, March 6). "Puppy Hell." Milwaukee Magazine. Retrieved from: https://www.milwaukeemag.com/PuppyHell/

Alfonsi, S. (2009, March 27). "Puppies Viewed as Livestock in Amish Community." ABC News. Retrieved from: https://abcnews.go.com/Business/story?id=7187712&page=1

Catherine, N. (2018, February 3). "The Amish and Animal Cruelty: An Unexpected Mix." Animal Advocate SPCA. Retrieved from: https://www.animaladvocatesscpa.com/blog/post/amish-animal-cruelty-unexpected-mix/

Block, K. & Amundson, S. (2021, May 10). "Our Horrible Hundred report exposes 100 puppy mills that sell to pet stores and online." Humane Society. Retrieved from: https://blog.humanesociety.org/2021/05/

horrible-hundred-report-exposes-100-puppy-mills-that-sell-to-pet-stores-and-online.html

Humane Society. (2022, May 9). "New report reveals licensed dog breeders still in business despite filthy conditions, dying dogs, and cruel practices." Retrieved from: https://www.humanesociety.org/news/new-report-reveals-licensed-dog-breeders-still-business-despite-filthy-conditions-dying-dogs.

DeNatale, D. & Miller, Corey (2021, May 11). "16 Ohio puppy mills listed on Humane Society 'Horrible Hundred' list." WKYC Studios. Retrieved from: https://www.wkyc.com/article/life/pets/ohio-has-16-puppy-mills-listed-humane-society-horrible-hundred-list/95-79bb052d-4bbd-4986-a516-337c9a6ae5c2

Goldfinger, D. (2020, June 19). "Dozens of dead dogs arrive at Toronto Pearson International Airport from Ukraine, CFIA says." Global News. Retrieved from: https://globalnews.ca/news/7086674/dead-puppies-toronto-pearson-airport-ukraine/

Block, K. (2018, May 25). "New Hampshire fight reveals American Kennel Club as champion of puppy mills not dogs." Humane Society. Retrieved from: https://blog.humanesociety.org/2018/05/new-hampshire-fight-reveals-american-kennel-club-champion-puppy-mills-not-dogs.html

Raining Cats and Dogs. (2014, March 11). "Why the AKC fights for puppy mills." Chicago Now. Retrieved from: https://www.chicagonow.com/raining-cats-dogs/2014/03/why-the-akc-fights-for-puppy-mills/

Worden, A. (2012, July 10). "Report: AKC opposes efforts to curb puppy mills, combat pet cruelty." *The Philadelphia Inquirer*. Retrieved from: https://www.inquirer.com/philly/blogs/pets/Report-AKC-opposes-efforts-to-curb-puppy-mills-combat-pet-cruelty.html

Weir, M., DVM & Buzhardt, L., DVM, (n.d.). "Designer Dog Breeds." VCA Animal Hospital. Retrieved from: https://vcacanada.com/know-your-pet/designer-dog-breeds

K9 Web. (n. d.) "What is the Difference Between an F1 and F1B Goldendoodle?" Retrieved from: https://www.k9web.com/breeds/f1-vs-f1b-goldendoodle/

Riviera Allergy Medical Center. (n. d.) "Is There Really Such a Thing as Hypoallergenic Dogs?" Retrieved from: https://www.rivieraallergy.com/blog/is-there-really-such-a-thing-as-hypoallergenic-dogs

Schimelpfening, Nancy, MS (2020, January 15) "Why There's No Such Thing as a Truly Hypoallergenic Dog." Healthline. Retrieved from: https://www.healthline.com/health-news/no-hypoallergenic-dogs

Kromash, Lori (2018, November 8). "The Art of Glueing Puppy Ears." Show Dog Store. Retrieved from: https://www.showdogstore.com/blog/the-art-of-glueing-puppy-ears/#:~:text=Ears%20should%20remain%20glued%20for,to%20take%20the%20ears%20down.

AKC Communications (2008, November 28) "AKC Statement on AVMA Crop and Dock policy." Retrieved from: https://www.akc.org/press-releases/akc-statement-on-avma-crop-and-dock-policy/

Originally printed in the American Kennel Club's In Session newsletter, Spring Issue 2011. "Issue Analysis: Dispelling the Myths of Cropped Ears, Docked Tails, Declaws, and Debarking." American Kennel Club. Retrieved from: https://images.akc.org/pdf/canine_legislation/Crop-Dock-Debark-Article.pdf

Chapter 4 – A Loving Forever Home

McAteer, A. (2011, August 1). "My rescue dog is perfect. But how long will this 'honeymoon' last?" The Globe and Mail. Retrieved from: https://www.theglobeandmail.com/life/relationships/my-rescue-dog-is-perfect-but-how-long-will-this-honeymoon-last/article626334/#:~:text=It'll%20show%20up%20in,TV%20or%20had%20an%20accident.

Danielle. (2021, November 13). "Phases of a Rescue Dog—Three Stages You Need to Know." Paws Leak. Retrieved from: https://pawleaks.com/phases-of-a-rescue-dog/

Phillips, J. (2021, April 8). "Gotcha Day: How to Celebrate Your Pet in 2021." Outward Hound. Retrieved from: https://outwardhound.com/furtropolis/fun/gotcha-day

Rescue Dogs 101. (n.d.). "18 Happy Gotcha Day Dog Ideas that your dog will do zoomies for!" Retrieved from: https://www.rescuedogs101.com/gotcha-day-dog/

Chapter 5 – Finding a Responsible Rescue

Animal Rescue Professionals. (2017, May 3). "How to Find a Reputable Animal Rescue." Retrieved from: https://www.animalrescueprofessionals.org/general-blog/slidefind-reputable-animal-rescue/

Hug A Bull. (n.d.). "Red Flags in Rescue." Retrieved from: https://www.hugabull.com/red-flags

Nathan J. Winograd. (n.d.). "No Kill 101." https://youtu.be/JCTt5JppNA8 Retrieved from: https://www.nathanwinograd.com/

Nathan J. Winograd. (2009) "Redemption: The Myth of Pet Overpopulation and The No Kill Revolution in America." Almaden.

Zelman, Joanna (2010, December 10) "PETA: 'Everyday Dogs' Ad Portrays Pets In Body Bags To Promote Adoption." Huffington Post. Retrieved from: https://www.huffpost.com/entry/peta-encourages-dog-adopt_n_794008

Thwartd video (2011, December 4) PETA Body Bags TV Commercial. Retrieved from: https://www.youtube.com/watch?v=wrdhkrWXKts

ABC15 – Arizona USA (2010, December 13) "PETA ad shows pets in body bags." ABC15-Arizona. Retrieved from: https://www.youtube.com/watch?v=vR2d5WkY1VU

PETA (2008, July 15) "Free Body Bag With Purchase of a Puppy." Retrieved from: https://www.peta.org/blog/free-body-bag-purchase-puppy/

Paws Abilities. (2012, March 19). "Responsible Rescues." Retrieved from: https://paws4udogs.wordpress.com/2012/03/19/responsible-rescues/

Reisen, J. (2019, November 8.). "How to Choose the Right Rescue Group." American Kennel Club. Retrieved from: https://www.akc.org/expert-advice/advice/how-to-choose-the-right-rescue-group/

Chapter 6 – Adopting a Special Needs Dog

Handicapped Pets. (2019, April 5). "Importance of Adopting a Special Needs Dog." Retrieved from: https://www.handicappedpets.com/blog/adopting-dog-with-special-needs/

Nolan, E. (n.d.). "Things to Consider Before Adopting a Special-Needs Dog." The Grey Muzzle Organization. Retrieved from: https://www.greymuzzle.org/grey-matters/adopting-senior-dog/things-consider-adopting-special-needs-dog

Sanders, Linley. (2021, January 22). "Who Saved Who? The Joy of Owning a Special Needs Pet." Daily Paws. Retrieved from: https://www.dailypaws.com/living-with-pets/pet-owner-relationship/the-joy-of-owning-a-special-needs-pet

Khuly, P. (2015, February 27). "6 Things You Should Do Before Adopting a Special Needs Pet." Vet Street. Retrieved From: http://www.vetstreet.com/our-pet-experts/6-things-you-should-do-before-adopting-a-special-needs-pet

Dog Tag Art. (n.d.). "Should You Adopt a Special Needs Pet?" Retrieved from: https://www.dogtagart.com/blog/should-you-adopt-special-needs-pet

Chapter 7 – The Canine Covid Crisis

Pearson, A. (2021, October 19). "Pandemic Puppies: Tackling A Growing Problem." *Forbes*. Retrieved from: https://www.forbes.com/uk/advisor/pet-insurance/pandemic-puppies/

Gagne, C. (2022, March 25). "Pandemic puppies have a major anxiety problem." *Macleans Magazine*. Retrieved from: https://www.macleans.ca/society/life/pandemic-puppies-have-a-major-anxiety-problem/

Reeder, J. (2022, March 22). "Untrained pandemic pups present dilemma for Americans." Today. Retrieved from: https://www.today.com/pets/untrained-pandemic-pups-present-dilemma-americans-t223603

Pierce, J. & Bekoff, M. (2021, October 26). "Home Alone: The Fate of Post Pandemic Dogs." *Scientific American*. Retrieved from: https://www.scientificamerican.com/article/home-alone-the-fate-of-postpandemic-dogs/

American Veterinarian Medical Association. (n.d.). "COVID-19." Retrieved from: https://www.avma.org/resources-tools/animal-health-and-welfare/covid-19

Clow, T. (2022, July 25). "Local SPCA Sees Influx of Dogs with Behavioural, Medical Issues. Radio Station 919 The Bend. Retrieved from: https://www.919thebend.ca/2022/07/25/118584/

Health for Animals. (n.d.). "Three ways COVID-19 has changed the veterinary profession." Retrieved from: https://www.healthforanimals.org/resources/newsletter/articles/three-ways-covid-19-has-changed-the-veterinary-profession/

Snyder, A. (2021, June 20). "COVID-19 pandemic magnifies workforce crisis in veterinary field." CNN. Retrieved from: https://www.cnn.com/2021/06/20/us/vet-tech-shortage-burnout/index.html

Sharkey, J. (2021, September 14). "The pandemic puppy craze is creating a veterinary crisis." Canadian Broadcast Corporation. Retrieved from: https://www.cbc.ca/news/canada/kitchener-waterloo/vet-shortage-veterinary-pandemic-puppy-1.6159143

United States Department of Agriculture. (2020, March 27). "Message to AWA Licensees and Registrants: Animal Care Inspections during COVID-19 Pandemic." Retrieved from: https://www.aphis.usda.gov/aphis/newsroom/stakeholder-info/stakeholder-messages/animal-care-news/status-of-ac-inspections-during-covid

United States Department of Agriculture. (2020, May 4). "Update. Message to AWA Licensees and Registrants: Animal Care Inspections during COVID-19 Pandemic." Retrieved from: https://www.usda.gov/media/press-releases/2020/03/17/usda-continues-focus-service-during-covid-19-outbreak

McQuillan, L. (2022, July 4). "Who gets Fluffy? Lawyers see spike in pet custody cases as couples split under pandemic pressure." Canadian Broadcast Corporation. Retrieved from: https://www.cbc.ca/news/canada/pet-custody-cases-rise-lawyers-say-1.6533847

Kale, S. (2022, July 16). Review. "You're not taking the dog! How pet custody battles turned nasty." The Guardian. Retrieved from: https://www.theguardian.com/lifeandstyle/2022/jul/16/youre-not-taking-the-dog-how-pet-custody-battles-turned-nasty

Chapter 8 – Talk Doggy to Me

Harvey, F. (2021, May 12). "Animals to be formally recognised as sentient beings." The Guardian. Retrieved from: https://www.theguardian.com/world/2021/may/12/animals-to-be-formally-recognised-as-sentient-beings-in-uk-law

Hodgson, S. (2015, December 4). "Re-Classifying Dogs as Sentient Beings: It's Time, America, It's Time." Huffington Post. Retrieved from: https://www.huffpost.com/entry/reclassifying-dogs-as-sen_b_8717888

Handwerk, B. (2018, August 15). "How Accurate Is the Theory of Dog Domestication in 'Alpha'." *Smithsonian Magazine*. Retrieved from: https://www.smithsonianmag.com/science-nature/how-wolves-really-became-dogs-180970014/

Morin, M. (2013, November 14). "When and where did dogs become our pets." *Los Angeles Times*. Retrieved from: https://www.latimes.com/science/sciencenow/la-xpm-2013-nov-14-la-sci-sn-dogs-domesticated-in-europe-20131114-story.html

Marshall, M. (2021, January 7). "Humans may have domesticated dogs by accident by sharing excess meat." *New Scientist*. Retrieved from: https://www.newscientist.com/article/2264329-humans-may-have-domesticated-dogs-by-accident-by-sharing-excess-meat/#:~:text=The%20timing%20and%20causes%20of,installed%20as%20pets%20by%20then.

Briggs, H. (2017, July 19). "How did dogs become our best friends? New Evidence." British Broadcasting Corporation. Retrieved from: https://www.bbc.com/news/science-environment-40638584

Kulkarnin, A. (2021, August 21). "Sniffer dogs trained at Vancouver Coastal Health can now detect COVID-19 on humans." Canadian Broadcasting Corporation. Retrieved from: https://www.cbc.ca/news/canada/british-columbia/covid-sniffer-dogs-1.6139254

The Conversation. (2022, February 9). "Dogs can be trained to sniff our COVID-19: A team of forensic researchers explain the science." Retrieved from: https://theconversation.com/dogs-can-be-trained-to-sniff-out-covid-19-a-team-of-forensic-researchers-explain-the-science-169012

Kramer, J. (2021, May 19.). "These sniffer dogs are learning to smell the coronavirus." *National Geographic Magazine*. Retrieved from: https://www.nationalgeographic.com/animals/article/see-dogs-trained-to-sniff-covid

ABOUT THE AUTHOR

Tracy Jessiman has been involved in dog rescue for over twenty years. She writes a weekly column about pet issues and rescue and is often sought out by local media for comments on animal abuse or pet-related legislation. For many years Jessiman highlighted homeless pets on local radio. She loves to cycle, bake, create new jam recipes and paint one-of-a-kind pet portraits. She lovingly donates all proceeds from her pet portraits to rescues. Jessiman has owned many wonderful rescue dogs and has fostered, transported, and advocated on their behalf. She has been rescuing animals most of her life, but she believes animals have rescued her.

Jessiman lives in Halifax, Nova Scotia, with her husband, Earl and their cherished rescue dog Sheena.

Printed in Canada